# A Christian "Selfie"

## A Pastor's Wife's Honest Look At Her Relationship With God

By:

## Jamie Walters

PRESS

*A Christian "Selfie"*
*A Pastor's Wife's Honest Look At Her Relationship With God*
by Jamie Walters

Printed in the United States of America

ISBN 9781498459167

www.xulonpress.com

To Sarah,

May you be blessed as you read!

Jamie Walters

# In Memory of:
# Dexter and Thea Clark

This book is dedicated to the memory of my parents

who exemplified the essence of unselfishness.

To my father, who taught me a work ethic and perseverance—

I am truly grateful. To my mother, because she was the most caring

and giving mother a daughter could have. I am humbled,

reflecting on how I never witnessed a selfish act on her behalf.

I only wish I could live up to her example!

# Contents

# Forward

When my loving mama came to me with a manuscript and said, "please read," I thought—what could I possibly add to a self-examining Christian book? After all, I haven't made time to fully read any of the books that my friends and family have given me on God, Prayer and relationships. When I'm not managing and editing commercial terms at work, I read scientific journals—because sometimes I feel my confidence can be more easily found in knowledge than faith. I pick up my Bible on whatever Sunday we successfully get our toddler out of the door without a meltdown.

Aside from failing to make time for the Bible and these inspirational books, my biggest shortcoming of all is taking a Selfie! No—really—either the photo is blurred because I've moved the hand holding the phone or my upper lip twitches as I get nervous, my eyes bug out or close, or in general, I just look like a crazy person. My selfies never quite look the way I want to look, or at the very least, how I see myself.

Like our Selfies, when we assess ourselves and our relationship with God, we will likely see that we require a good amount of editing.

Isn't it amazing, though, how God has blessed us with the Bible, throughout which we are reminded that God loves us for who we are—unedited—but wants us to be better and walk with Him. God loves me with my twitchy upper lip, buggy eyes and all my other flaws. He loves me, but God challenges me to edit, to make the corrections so that my life can be more fulfilling.

I really did not let my need to "edit" myself and my relationship with God, sink in until reading my mother's manuscript. I found that a fulfilling life is quite different from a self-fulfilling one. My parents, with the world's influence, armed me with scriptures and enough philosophical and social concepts to talk my way through just about any conversation related to God—at least a conversation related to God at a cocktail party. But the common lesson ends there. While my parents armed me with prayer and the importance of a relationship with God, the world taught me that I could do it on my own. That as long as I protected myself, respected myself and worked very hard to be the best person I wanted to be, I would succeed. I do succeed, but my Selfie is a wreck. I never once—on any particular day—considered what my life would be like if I really assessed this flawed Selfie and "edited" my relationship with God. At least until now—until reading this book!

I want you to read it—to see how a woman who would experience life-altering events like family medical disorders, numerous relocations, church conflicts, heart-wrenching challenges with her children and devastating realizations, would come out of it all smiling. Only by the surrender of her **self,** only by examining **her (self,)** only by constant editing and revision to have a more thoughtful relationship with God, could she have survived. And, not only has she survived, she loves and rejoices each and every day.

That's the Selfie we want. . .one that glistens and needs so little refining, because it *studies and shows itself approved.*

# Introduction

I am going to take you on a journey. There are many pictures of my life I want to share with you. I begin my story with a small glimpse of my college life as a babe in Christ and travel across many years of learning, with God's help, how to stay in God's Word and do His will. I have not arrived. It is my prayer that you will gain an understanding of how my failures and successes became strength in the Lord as I depended on Him. To do this, I needed to take a "Selfie" of my life and share with you. Believe me, I have had past failures that seemed impossible to face. I have cried and anguished over raising three girls. I have also laughed with and immensely loved those same three daughters. Without fail, God picked me up and taught me to depend on Him during those moments of anguish. Did I always listen? No. Unfortunately, I am probably no different than most of you. It takes me several tries to find God's perfect will for my life. You see, I am basically plagued with a selfish nature. Have you ever sung the very old hymn, "I Surrender All," yet, don't? You could have the same struggle. That is why you need to take this journey with me. On this journey, we are going to learn how we can overcome selfishness in todays' world. You might question, "Do I even want to try to overcome my own selfishness?"

Let's face it. My generation, the Baby Boomers, brought to the sixties the thought of "free love" and "live life to the fullest!" We successfully established selfishness through our lyrics, television programing, literature or other written media and movies. In the seventies, came the phrases that put down friends like "psyche" or "in your face." The eighties and nineties were no better with phrases like "bite me" or "eat my shorts." These phrases indicated a selfish demeanor that presented a cruel side of humanity that has only escalated in recent years. You may or may not be aware of the escalation of bullying and "cutting" going on with today's youth. As a middle school teacher, I personally witnessed many young people abusing their own bodies. I have personally witnessed adults/parents teaching their children to hit others if they hit you. Oh, I know it would seem many are just teaching them to defend themselves. If you have read the Bible, Jesus tells us to turn the other cheek and use words of love and understanding when in conflict with others. Did I always do this as a young Christian? No. I gave into selfish ways on a daily basis. Now that I am older and somewhat wiser, I start my day with Bible study and prayer. I have learned it is easier to get rid of those selfish tendencies. However, it doesn't matter what your age is, what matters is your walk with the Lord. As you read the following chapters, you will learn how to resolve the earthly issues of selfishness through self-reflection. It is so easy for you and me to get caught up in selfish behavior. What about the guy who took your parking place and you even had your blinker on? Does he/she deserve finger gestures and a cursing? Selfishness! We see it constantly in our daily lives from line breaking to stealing, and yes, even murder.

As a middle school teacher, I was on my way to school one morning when I changed lanes (with my blinker on) and the person behind me flashed their bright lights. They zoomed up beside me and proceeded to run me off the road! I was very scared and praised the Lord for the unoccupied turning lane. I braked hard as the van sped by, avoiding a near accident. I'm sure you have had similar experiences you could convey here.

Humanity has a flawed "selfie." From recent stories in Ferguson, Missouri to the crisis in the Middle East, we see the selfish desires of humanity. Presently, it seems our world is on a fast track of self-seeking cravings here on earth. The selfish acts of our leaders and role models have appalled the Christian community. This occurrence coupled with all the violence against our fellow human beings, have again started the rumblings of the second coming of Christ. We definitely do not know the hour when Jesus will return. Will we as individuals be ready? How can we possibly overcome this selfishness? There is only one way we can overcome selfishness and it begins with me living daily for Jesus. It begins with **you living daily for Jesus!** Our selfish desires prohibit us from that personal relationship with Jesus. We all need the love of Jesus within us to overcome our selfish desires. I am writing this book to show you how you can overcome those little issues of selfishness that can become compounded to take our joy away from daily living. When we overcome selfishness, there is joy in the Lord. This joy can shatter our selfish desires.

I would like to share with you several concepts that I have found through scriptures that can enable you to live a compassionate and giving life in an extremely selfish world. In order to do this, I address the need for you to flee from the bondage of sin in your daily life. You and I can do this when we start each day by renewing our minds. We must be transformed daily to have a relationship with the Lord. I have included a chapter on identifying your God given gifts. So many of God's children do not know what gifts they possess. You may not really know what gifts you possess. It is my prayer that as you study and read this chapter, God will reveal to you how you can best serve Him. Study on the scriptures given so that you can give God your total service. You may need to examine your true nature and ask God to help you with your self-centeredness. To do this, you can learn to pray without ceasing. I know. . .I struggle with this daily as well. But in all things, you must take your petitions to God so that He can bless you. It is then that you need to learn how to value yourself and realize you are a child of God. You will become truly blessed as you learn **you** have value. Accordingly, from those blessings, you can learn to rejoice in the Lord, always! It is my prayer that you can live each day rejoicing in all circumstances. You are called to rejoice in the good times and in the times of trials. I am making a conscious effort to practice rejoicing daily. Try it! Meditate on rejoicing no matter how you feel. You can't help but feel better! You will overcome selfishness! You will have joy in the Lord!

Please use the lines I have given you throughout the book to meditate, pray and write down thoughts that will give you peace and joy as you search your heart. May God bless you as you take your "Selfie."

# Chapter One

# Adam and Eve. . .In the Beginning

"Instead you ought to say, 'If the Lord wills, we shall live and do this or that." (James 4:15*NKJV*)

I n the beginning, I created Man:

1. Handsome (preferably a football player)
2. Non-smoker
3. Christian
4. Future Preacher

College life was hectic, but so much fun! I loved going to the football games on warm sunny Saturday afternoons and cheering on my better-than-average college team. I grew up in North Alabama during the Bear Bryant era of football, and I even played the grueling game of "powder-puff" football for four years at my local high school. I was a tight end and fast as lightning! But that is another story. Truth be told, there was perhaps only one thing more exciting in life than watching and playing football: thinking about "Adam," the man of my prayers. Sitting directly behind me in my "Teaching Elementary Physical Education" class—molded directly from God's clay—was a rather handsome young man. Well. . .that is, if one could get past the splinted broken nose that had purplish, black eyes peering out at me. My heart melted at his smile that was straight from some "Crest" toothpaste commercial. He was a freshman outside linebacker on the Jacksonville State University Gamecock team that I cheered for both home and away. Not many students went to the away games, but my roommates and I were very devoted Gamecock fans. So, it was only natural that I was interested in him when I found out he was on the football team. I could check off number one from my "Adam" prayer list: Handsome (preferably a football player.) On our very first date I found out he was a non-smoker and a Christian. Check one, two, and three!

Seriously, I had offered this prayer request up to the Lord. When I was in high school, I attended a Christian youth camp where I had prayed that I would meet a young Christian man who loved the Lord like I did, and would want to become a pastor someday. Oh, and he could not be a smoker! My friends always laughed at my requests, but I knew that if I wanted those to come true, I had to make my requests known to the Lord. (Phil. 4:6 my paraphrase)

In the early days of my Christian walk, I prayed as an immature Christian. Truth be told, I was not praying daily either. I also lifted up very selfish prayers. While my trust in the Lord was great, and my prayer for a future Christian husband genuine, I prayed for a future on my terms, not God's terms. There is a reason why I gave you the scripture to read at the beginning of this chapter: what follows in this book is both a story of my life, and my transitioning from a self-centered life to a God-centered one. Learning to pray in God's will is paramount to my transformation as a Christian, and is the only thing that held me closer to God and my family while navigating through life's deepest challenges. It is my prayer, as you read these pages, that you too will learn to pray in God's will. I just want you to understand that I am no different from most Christians—I rush into the presence of God with selfish desires that I think of as needs. I found through soul-searching Bible studies and constant prayer how I could reflect upon past challenges and share how a relationship with God can give you true joy. Please keep this in mind as you read about my journey. You will see that there are times where I was truly walking in God's will and those times when it is evident I struggled. You just might want to take a "selfie" of your prayer life as well.

My high school camp days were the beginning of a wonderful relationship with my God. Those fun-filled college days were the beginning of a life-long commitment with my future husband, David. (Hey, it may not be "Adam", but it's Biblical!) Life, however, is not cloaked in the warmth, cheer, and love of Christian camp; there would be many "rocky mountains" to climb and treacherous valleys that we would traverse as well. That is why I felt such an overwhelming desire to navigate you through forty plus years of life yearning to please both the Lord and my husband. When I look back, I am in awe of the marvelous grace given me by God to endure the hardships, triumphs, and successes that only Jesus can give. I would like to share with you several truths that God gave me. It is my prayer that these truths might help you as you journey through your life with God, your husband or friend, your children, or your life as a pastor's wife. No matter where you are in your walk with the Lord, or if you really are not sure you have been walking with God at all, He will bless you as you read and answer some simple truths about yourself.

Do you struggle with who you are or what you are becoming? I was conflicted as well—too caught up in what I wanted. As a young believer, I was finding it hard to listen to what God wanted me to become. Did you let that sink in? Oh, there was no doubt I wanted to be a follower of the cross. I just was selfish enough to want what I wanted on "**My**" terms! Fortunately, God showed grace and humor.

Here is a truth—an "Adam" prayer is the least of all prayers we must lift up. I was too young and naïve to understand just how much I must stay in prayer for such a request. That young man that I met in college had no idea what I was praying for him. If he had known my prayer, he would have never gone on that first date! Life is dynamic and there is a reason they say, "Walk with the Lord." Even though my husband was a Christian, he would spend several years running from the task God had for him. The Lord would teach me that I would need to continue in prayer and listen to Him. There is a scripture from 1 Corinthians that would help me understand everything I attempted to do should be done to God's glory. "Therefore, whether you eat or drink, or whatever you do, do all to the glory of God." (1 Corinthians 10:31 NKJV) It would take me years of searching after God's heart and

His will for my life before I fully understood how to do this. I learned that I needed to get into a quiet place without distractions in order to listen to God's will. To have a relationship with God, you must talk to Him! I discovered early that I was to "Be anxious for nothing, but in everything by prayer and supplication, with thanksgiving, let your requests be made known to God;" (Philippians 4:6 NKJV) I was to let God know what I needed and thank Him for his answer. I prayed about my first job. Do you pray? You may need to pray about your relationship with whom you are dating or married. It could be that you need to pray about your work place. Need a job? Pray about it! It could be goals you need to accomplish. Better yet, you may need to set goals for a closer walk with the Lord. "For the Holy Spirit will teach you in that very hour what you ought to say." (Luke 12:12 NKJV) Isn't that a great comfort? There have been so many times I exclaimed to the Lord that I did not know how to pray. Find your quiet place and remember to pray in God's will. I am giving you a few lines to write out **your** (*Philippians 4:6)* prayer requests. After you have had your prayer time, read chapter two. You will find out how to listen to God's small voice.

_____

_____

_____

_____

_____

_____

# Chapter Two

# Swallowed By A Whale

"Then Paul stood up, and motioning with his hand said, 'Men of Israel, and you who fear God, listen;" (Acts 13:15 NKJV)

"Why do you not understand My speech? Because you are not able to listen to My word." (John 8:43 NKJV)

The first several years of our marriage I like to think I listened to God's voice more often than not. David and I were young and in love. I was faithfully attending a Methodist church, and when I could convince him, David would join me. He had grown up as a Baptist. Both of us were teaching and coaching. David spent a majority of his time coaching football. You can probably imagine the drill (pun intended.) There were coaches meetings, team meetings, public relations, scouting teams, teaching football skills, and I cannot leave out game days. I was lucky to see him at 11:00 at night! Likewise, I also was coaching tennis and had a cheerleading squad that occupied my time at a different school. I felt like we were leading two separate lives. You may probably feel some of the same pressures that living life is dealing you. I can remember wanting to be at the same school so we could go to events together. The louder the noise grew from these activities, the more silent God was for us. The more we listened to our teams, fans and administrators, the less we listened to God. Now, I'm not saying you can't do these things while serving the Lord. But, we were running nonstop! We were just on our feet and not on our knees! Routines turned into motions. Tasks turned into chaos. The calendar filled up until the only spot empty was our hearts, which had placed God on a back shelf. There we were—Christians who had stopped listening and were lost at sea. Do you feel like you are drowning in the affairs of this world? Are you listening to the still small voice that guides you from right and wrong? Are you being swallowed by the "whale?"

God retrieves his lost sheep in one way or another. . .Jonah was swallowed by a whale then spewed out for service to God. God's retrieval of David and me came in the form of a Tupperware party. My friend had invited me to her Tupperware party and David, feeling sorry for her husband having to endure the torture of so many women in his home, invited him to our house to hang out. The friend explained to David that he was going to a revival at a local church that night and he wanted David to come along. David replied he had something that he was doing and wouldn't be able to go. The friend quickly retorted, "David, didn't you just invite me to your house to hang out?"

David had been had!

Doesn't God have a wonderful sense of humor?

So, while I sorted through plastic containers, David went to the revival and came home a changed man! He barged through the door that night excited, and wanted us both to go to the revival the next night. He even told me that he wanted me to become a Baptist! Surely he had misunderstood God! I was a good little Methodist girl who never considered becoming a Baptist. Matter of fact, I had always assumed he would join with me in the Methodist church. I reluctantly agreed to go, but resolved in my heart that I would not change religious affiliations. I must admit, I was selfish!

That night, God had a different agenda. He touched my heart in such a way that I knew I was to go forward at the invitation and not only rededicate my life to Him, but also join the Baptist church and be united with my spouse. David was very surprised when I grabbed his hand and said, "Come on!" I could hardly contain my excitement knowing that God had intervened to put us back on course for His purpose—not mine!

We both began to serve the Lord fervently. We visited people and invited them to church and grew through participation in outreach programs and Bible studies. David and I began to grow as one when we listened to Him. That was the key—listening to God. Are you listening to God? Or, have you been swallowed by the whale of life? Are you just sitting there waiting for someone to save you? Like the scripture at the beginning of this chapter, are you not able to listen to God's voice? Are you so caught up in living life that you are "deaf" to God's call? I'm giving you a few lines to write your requests and if need be, ask God's forgiveness for neglecting His call to walk with Him. It could be you aren't sure Jesus lives in your heart. Romans 3:23 tells us that all have sinned and come short of the glory of God. We are also promised in Romans 10:9 that if we confess our sins to the Lord Jesus and believe God has raised Him from the dead, we will be saved. Pray for God to cleanse you from your sin. Write down a plan of action to talk regularly to God and read His Word and listen. You will need to make the time in your schedule. It is like making the time to exercise or even eat. It has to be scheduled at first until it becomes a part of your life. First, make a place/location to regularly pray to God. Second, make a time that meets your needs so that you can consistently meet God and pray. You may have to get up early or it could be that your best time is after the kids are in bed and you can sit in solitude in a quiet place. Make your schedule here. My prayer is that you succeed!

_____

_____

_____

_____

_____

_____

# Chapter Three

## Lazarus, Come Forth!

"Your word I have hidden in my heart, That I might not sin against You." (Psalm 119:11 NKJV)

"I will not forget Your word." (Psalm 119:16 NKJV)

David and I had been married for almost four years and he still had not helped me check off that "Pastor" requirement from my Adam list. He was still coaching football. His "ministry" at this time was bringing young men to Christ through the Fellowship of Christian Athletes. David contacted businesses, churches and civic clubs to send athletes to FCA camp. We were also involved with teaching weekly Sunday school classes, youth activities, and choir. We thought our life together was almost perfect, except for one thing—children.

So, my perfectly manly, football-coaching husband and I began praying for a child. God finally blessed us with a child just as I was becoming nervous and impatient. And imparting His wonderful sense of humor—God gave us, not only one daughter, He gave us three daughters in four short years! Perfect. . .right? Well, I sure thought it was! Three little girls to dress up and curl their hair and take to dance and gymnastics lessons were such a joy for me. It was such a blessing to watch them grow and have so much fun with each other. The childhood years were wonderful! Unfortunately, no one warned me about puberty! We'll discuss this later. . .

We were living in Kentucky when all three girls were born. However, as is the case with many football coaches, we moved from Glasgow to Bardstown to Clinton County to follow David's career. That meant packing up our household possessions and then unpacking. It meant leaving dear friends and sometimes relatives. It was a very good thing that the Lord blessed me with an easily adaptable personality. I made new friends easily. Our third move brought David the head football job in Clinton County. After giving birth to our third daughter, I started leading an exercise class and teaching gymnastics in an old building that I rented. I wanted to get my body back into shape, so I led a combined ladies Bible study class and "Zumba" style (Jazzercise) class in the old building after my gymnastic classes. David and I were very happy during our time here, but our faith would be put to the ultimate test.

The water lines in our community had broken overnight. For public safety concerns, they had to call off school. We decided to go visit David's sister, Judy, who lived about sixty miles away. As we walked in her door, a bombshell hit us. David could not get inside his sister's home by himself. He became paralyzed on one side and could not talk plainly either. He complained that he was seeing in multiples. A perfectly healthy man of thirty was suffering the symptoms of a full-fledge stroke! I became paralyzed with fear! My sister-in-law called for her husband to come. The hospital there said he had to be transported in an ambulance as I tried to calm my two little girls and feed my newborn baby. I vaguely remember asking Judy to take care of my three little girls as I jumped in the ambulance and anxiously prayed as I had never prayed before. I prayed for the entire thirty minute ride and my prayer went something like this: "Lord, help me to accept your will. I don't know how I can raise three little girls and take care of a husband who is paralyzed and can no longer work! I am placing us in your care, Lord. Forgive me for my selfishness. . .David does not have to be your servant in the pulpit if that is not your will. Just save him." I prayed in earnest.

Suddenly, a peace and calm that I cannot explain came over me. As we walked inside that emergency room, I knew that whatever the outcome, Jesus was there with me, holding my hand. I followed the whole group working on David into the emergency room and listened as the doctors said he was totally paralyzed on the right side of his body. I listened as David tried to talk and only gibberish was coming out of his mouth. I managed to get close enough to grab hold of his hand and pray silently as they continued to work. I was brought back into the room from my prayers when the doctor said, "What are you doing in here? You are not supposed to be in here!" I looked him in the eye and said, "My husband is going to be alright. God has a pur-pose for his life and God will heal him." The doctor looked me in the eyes and said that he was glad I had faith and that I would need it in the days ahead. He gruffly pronounced that my husband had suffered a major stroke and was paralyzed on his right side, could not talk, and could not see plainly. He needed me to leave so they could get David completely stabilized and he coldly reminded me that I needed to fill out paperwork for admittance into their hospital. I walked out of that ER and went straight to the hospital chapel where I broke down and cried. Yes, the doctor had placed fear in my heart. My comfort was gone when I gave way to fear. However, I did not wallow in my fear for long. I found a Gideon Bible on the pew and picked it up and turned to several different scripture passages that began to bring me comfort. I had not forgotten God's Word. What I quoted at the beginning of the chapter became real (Psalm 119:16.) Consequently, as I read scripture after scripture, Jesus flooded my soul and wrapped His arms around me and again gave me that peace that passes all understanding. 2 Corinthians 12:9 jumped out at me. God promised me that His grace was sufficient for me because His strength was made perfect in my weakness. After reading this scripture, I kept repeating Philippians 4:13. Christ was strengthening me. After I spent time praying for David in his hospital room, I left the hospital with my brother-in-law to go and give my little girls the love and comfort that I knew they were waiting for. Praise God they were too small to ask too many questions. Our eldest daughter was already asking, "Mommy, why was Daddy talking funny like he was just a kid?" I eased their minds with prayer time for their daddy and I put them to bed.

The next day, I drove the thirty miles to the hospital praying for a miracle. The sun was unusually bright and I got there without even knowing how I got there! I was fervently praying and praising God as I drove. As I walked down the hall to David's room, I could hear him talking to the nurse. Praise the Lord! He was talking slowly and with difficulty, but I could understand what he was saying! When I entered the room, he was telling the nurse that he was no longer seeing multiples but that his vision was blurred. I rushed to his bed and exclaimed God had answered our prayers. We received a miracle! Not only had he been out of bed to use the bathroom, the nurse told me that he attempted to enter the hallway with all kinds of monitors on him trying to find a way out! He was quickly put back into bed by the hospital staff. The next few days of me traveling back and forth to the hospital from my sister-in-law's home seemed a blur to me. I was trying to take care of a newborn, play with my two little girls, and visit with my husband to rejoice about his progress. David did progress beyond what the doctors thought was possible! The doctor commented that he guessed he was going to have to record on his medical records that David had suffered a severe migraine headache. He had never had a patient that was paralyzed from a stroke recover and walk the next morning. He was baffled. All the tests he ran were inconclusive. The doctor summarized his diagnosis with me, "I guess I've seen a miracle." I confirmed that he had, in fact, witnessed a miracle and that we should Praise God for it!

There were some effects from that "stroke" that took longer to heal. David could not taste his food for almost six months. He doused his food in pepper, but to no avail! He sure did sneeze a lot, but he never tasted his food! His visual depth perception was dramatically impaired. His hearing was magnified. It was as if a whole room of individuals were talking when in reality, only two were speaking. To this day, he hears things that I cannot hear at all. I often have to remind him to talk slower as he talks faster than he ever did before that day.

All of these side effects caused him a tremendous amount of anxiety during the months ahead. As the days passed, he became more anxious to return to school and coaching. He was not a happy camper staying at home! The stroke had happened on February 1, 1982. Gradually, his physical functioning was returning, but still, he had not recovered his taste, normal vision, or normal hearing. In his mind, he was more than ready to return to school. I did not believe he was ready and I told him he did not need to return to school. That is when David told me to invite Art (a surgeon friend) and his wife, Tammy, over for dinner. David said, "If Art tells me I can go back to school, you have to shut up and be quiet!"

Art and Tammy came over for dinner. After dinner, Art looked at David and asked him if he understood how blessed he was to have been given God's grace? David answered, "What do you mean, Art?" Art proceeded to explain how he knew David had been running from God's will. He told David, "God had to allow you to be slowed down to get your attention!" He shared that David and I needed to pray and ask for God to show us His will. . ."And, NO, you cannot go back to school yet!" David definitely did not want to hear that last part. I was wondering if he had heard the first part when Art continued to share his wisdom. He said, "David, what you experienced was a miracle and medically we cannot explain what happened to you. I believe that God allowed you to be slowed down to get you to realize He has something better for both you and Jamie." Art believed that God had spared David for His service—we needed to find out what that service was.

Have you ever had someone come to you and talk to you like that? Art was not only a friend, but he had served as our Angel on earth. God sent Art into our lives to draw David's attention toward the need for a searching prayer for God's will in David's life. I would love to tell you that he made the commitment to enter into God's ministry that very night. He did not. We did talk about what Art had said and prayed together that night before bedtime. David shared later with me that he had been running from the Lord since before we met. He said that when he was seventeen his father was talking to him and stated, "Son, I want you to be happy playing college ball if that is what you want. I want you to play ball for you, not me. And, if you want to go into the ministry, it is okay with me." David shared with me he had no idea why his father said that. At the time, he chose to run further away from the ministry. He also shared that there were a series of events that happened to cause him to run away from a deeper commitment to God. Before the stroke, David had coached a young man whom he tremendously respected. Patrick was a special young man who loved the Lord. On Easter Eve, Patrick was killed in an automobile accident. The young people in the school were devastated and David counseled with many of them. (I might add he wasn't even a counselor yet!) There were decisions made for the Lord as a result of Patrick's life and His walk with the Lord. David shared he was moved by the faith of Patrick's parents, yet he was not ready to make the commitment to follow God's will.

I cannot explain God's opening and closing of doors, but what I will say is that God knows our heart. God knows that his people will do what is necessary to get back to God's will for them. In addition to the stroke and sending Art into David's life, God closed the door to David's football program. David had explained to the superintendent that to expand the football program money was needed or they should probably dissolve the program. In early May, the superintendent would not commit the funds to meet the demands of an expanding program. David had finally returned to work in late April, and less than a month later, he was suddenly jobless. What would David and I do? He wasn't even fully healed. Where would we go to recover and 'resurrect' our life plans? It meant moving once again.

Desperate and with no work promised, we asked my parents if we could move into their home until David could find work and we could find a home. I had built a gymnastics business in Kentucky and we agreed we could do the same in my hometown. What a humbling experience. And, what love my parents had when they agreed to receive their daughter with a husband and three little girls! In August, two months after David had the football program dissolved, we loaded up our meager possessions and gymnastics equipment into a rented cattle truck and I drove the girls to Alabama in the backseat of my Volkswagen bug.

As it turns out, I was going home. . .

To my sweet home Alabama!

We added five people to my parent's small, 1300 square foot home! We definitely prayed together every day as we embarked on this journey. We did not pray for a ministry. We did not pray for a job for David at the time. We did pray for God to show us what He wanted, and for me to be blessed with a gymnastics business in my hometown. There was an old car dealership building on the main street of my hometown. It was in bad shape and an eye sore. When we approached the owner with the idea of us fixing up his building, painting the outside, and what we thought we could afford as a monthly payment, he agreed. We were praying about all of our endeavors and God was blessing our efforts. The Holy Spirit was teaching us how to pray more effectively. Meanwhile, God was healing David's body. Hard work and my mother's southern cooking seemed to resurrect David's taste-buds. He began to eat everything in sight!

The townspeople took notice of a young couple repairing and painting and making that "eye sore" look really nice. My mother, David, and I sewed curtains to span approximately eighty feet across the front so that passers-by could not see the children as they learned in their classes. The building was so spacious we were able to purchase a used floor exercise spring floor and were able to offer Class IV and III competitive gymnastics. Our girls have such fond memories of the Balance Beam. They not only learned gymnastic skills, they had birthday parties and friends over to play and have so much fun.

Just as God brought forth Lazarus (John 11,) God was bringing us forth to a new Christian walk. We decided to join the local Baptist church and immediately found many God-led friends who helped us grow deeper in our commitment to the Lord and becoming disciples. We had the confidence that we could ask anything in God's will and he would hear us. (1 John 14-15 NKJV) We believed all things would work together for us. (Philippians 4:13 NKJV)

David needed one college course to finish his first master's degree. He was looking to become a regional director in FCA. Unknown to us, God had willed him a position coaching football again. He told the man offering him the job that he was looking at a position serving in FCA and that he really did not want to go back to school. David did not want to be a student again. His friend told him that he would have a greater influence if he would just become a counselor and football coach for him. He certainly did not want to pay for more college with no job and three girls to support. We did not understand how God was working through it all to place David into His will again. God made it possible for David to get his counseling certification by opening up an internship in counseling at the University of Alabama. Just like Jonah, David was hesitant to make that commitment to be in God's will of going back to school. But, the internship made the task much more fun and exciting. God was preparing David to become a counselor.

David was satisfied and joyous in his service at that time. We both knew we were in God's will and at peace in our service to the Lord. The thought of David becoming a pastor was not even in my mind. He was speaking as a Gideon and as an FCA speaker in many local churches. I was coaching and teaching gymnastics and serving in the Gideon Auxiliary.

Have you ever run away from a task or commitment that you made? It is time to reflect upon your own walk with the Lord. Are you allowing him to bring you forth for service? Are you running away from serving the Lord where he wants you? Sometimes, God has to take you on a journey to broaden your horizons so He can prepare you for His service. Get into God's Word and search for a peace that passes all understanding on the task you are thinking about. Jot down what "you think" God would have you do. Now, pray diligently to make sure you are seeking God's will rather than your own personal interest.

_____

_____

_____

_____

_____

_____

God placed people into our lives that taught us how to get into God's word and search the scriptures. We became involved in the Master Life Program and learned to hide scriptures in our hearts. All of us should take the time to memorize scriptures. I challenge you to try and memorize at least one scripture verse per week. You will be blessed. Your joy will become complete! The Psalmist knew that when you hide God's Word in your heart, you will be sustained and satisfied. You can live a new life that God brings forth from your heart. We see this when Jesus commanded Lazarus to come forth from death. Lazarus began a new life with Jesus. You can also claim that new life in Christ.

We began to look for a home to buy. My parents even approached us with not moving out at all and expanding their home by buying the vacant lot next to them. That sounded like a good option. Again, we had a hiccough! After two years of David counseling, coaching and working with FCA , the journey seemed to end. State funding once again left David without the counseling position. David did not want to stay in coaching at the time. Although we did not understand, God was still in control. David shared with me later he began to question what God had in store for him. Ironically, David chose to make a living as a carpenter to put food on the table. Yes, God was allowing David to gain invaluable building experience that would serve him not only building physical structures, but in building God's kingdom. He built anything from lake peers to large plush jewelry boxes. He even remodeled a chain bank in our community. David had been "brought forth." Just like Lazarus, he had been given a new life of service. God was also blessing and utilizing us more in the Gideon ministry. What a blessing! I cannot begin to describe on paper the daily joys that the Gideon ministry brought to both of us. Through the Gideon ministry, David and I had the prayer support of many dedicated men and women to encourage us. When the Lord closed the door on high school athletics, David believed that God was preparing him for a counseling position in college athletics as an academic athletic counselor. We were praying and asking God to direct us and give David a vision for what God's will in our lives might be. David and I felt since he had been privileged to be on the counseling staff in a major Southern University that he could serve on a college athletic staff as an academic athletic advisor. He prepared resumes of his work and life experiences with FCA and college counseling to send out to several universities where he had contacts. While I was planning events for giving away Gideon testaments, David was in communication with a college athletic director in a major southwestern university for a possible position. He shared with me later that he had talked to God and asked why he had been given all the experience in athletic counseling if that wasn't what God wanted him to do. David had been given so many experiences that seemed to be pointing to the type of service that he had to offer in being an athletic counselor. What we didn't know is that God was preparing David for a higher calling.

During this time, I was working at The Balance Beam, leading Bible studies, and participating with the Gideon Auxiliary. Not only were we in God's Word, we were taking the Word and giving it away. Service to God became our priority. David began praying about the possibility of the college athletic director position coming available. We became excited about the potential opportunities. Again, God closed doors that we thought were opening because it was not His will. The position never materialized and we worked all the harder at the ministries we were engaging. We were extremely disappointed. We questioned why David had been given so many gifts and yet he had not received direction for using those gifts.

At church, our minister of music encouraged me to sing solo. I was scared to death! Being in the Word gave me the boldness to do that. I had always sung in the church choir and loved that service to God. Nevertheless, God once again, gave me a calm spirit and I began to sing for Him. I began to lead a Bible study class in the gymnastics building

I rented. It became the will of God that I take the leadership role of serving as WMU director in our church. I was as busy as I had ever been, but I was busy for the Lord and He was blessing me and my family as we had never been blessed before. I discovered Galatians 5:16 and claimed it to rid myself of selfishness. Paul tells us that when we walk in the Spirit, we cannot walk in the flesh. It seemed we were right where the Lord wanted us. God was preparing me to be a pastor's wife.

It was during this time, that I was involved with a group of ladies who felt called to anoint a great prayer warrior of God. Our friend and prayer companion was diagnosed with a brain tumor and the doctors had given her only a couple of months to live. Our prayer group went to our friends' bedside, anointed her with oil, and we prayed. Together, in one accord, we prayed, if it be God's will, in the name of Jesus, He would take her brain tumor and dry it up. We believed faithfully and claimed Matthew 21:22 that we could ask anything in prayer and receive it. After we finished praying, our friend said that she felt cleansed! Within the week, another MRI had been administered with new results found. Praise the Lord—there was no tumor! Our friend had just experienced a miracle and I had now witnessed two such instances. If I had not been a believer of miracles before, there was absolutely no question as to God's healing powers in answer to prayer. Many people came to know the Lord through her testimony of healing. Our Bible study groups grew tremendously. We studied God's Word fervently and non-believers became believers. Again, God was preparing me to be a pastor's wife.

Accordingly, as David spent more time in God's Word—it did not return void. Actually, it was not the Bible David read, but a Christian publication that came to my parents' home with David's name on it. He had never received that publication before and we have never seen it since. We look back and believe God had sent it so that David could read one article in it dealing with God's call into the ministry. He became convicted that he should enter the ministry and that night we prayed for God's will in David becoming a pastor. The next Sunday, I looked up to see David walking down the aisle of our church. I was humbled as our preacher declared to the church congregation that David had surrendered his heart and life to God's calling of the church ministry. This IS what I had prayed for, right? Too many years had passed since my "Adam" list. By now, I had grown accustomed to the service in the Gideon Auxiliary, WMU, and many other activities in our church. Selfishness began to enter my thoughts. How dare David leave the Gideon ministry just when I was being so fulfilled by this work! I didn't want to be a preacher's wife so bad that we would have to leave this wonderful ministry and David would become a REAL minister! Was I being selfish? You bet cha! I was allowing selfishness to creep back into my life. I did not recognize this at the time. When we have selfish wants and desires, do we ever recognize our folly? Rarely! That is why Satan can get such a hold on us. We don't even realize we are being selfish.

I have realized over the years of service to the Lord that it is easy to serve the Lord in the church and still be very selfish. Church committees can disagree on so many issues and cause splits between factions based on selfish desires of a few individuals. I am amazed at how Satan can blind these individuals to their selfish ways. Just like me being selfish over what I wanted, others do not realize their selfish wants and desires and are filled with animosity toward those who think differently. Have you ever had this happen to you? Maybe you are taking a "selfie" and are just now realizing how selfish you have been over an issue in your church or with your spouse or family member. Here are a few lines to give the Lord your selfish desires so that you can serve Him and become more Christ like. Look deep inside. Bind Satan away so you can see where you may be hiding selfish desires. Or, it could be you are out of God's will and you need to write down possible ideas that the Lord will give you as you listen to Him. Search for the Lord's guidance for your life. Write your prayer here:

_____

_____

_____

_____

_____

_____

# Chapter Four

# Exodus. . .Follow The Truth

". . .but, speaking the truth in love, may grow up in all things into Him who is the head—Christ—" (Ephesians 4:15 NKJV)

The Lord had not abandoned me. He sent several very sweet ladies to pray with me and help me realize that God was calling my husband and that he needed my support and prayers as well. David enrolled into seminary classes through the New Orleans extension in Birmingham, Alabama. We were praying for guidance and I began to realize that I should become a spiritual helpmate of encouragement. The minister of education at our church was being called away from his ministry and he asked David to take on various responsibilities that he was performing. God was preparing David for what would come next. Shortly after David enrolled in seminary, he was approached by his hometown church in Kentucky to be the Minister of Education and Youth. He said he would come up to make some suggestions to them as he really wasn't interested in coming back to his hometown. We made the journey back to his hometown to attend a football game and talk with them about the needs in youth ministry. It was during this meeting that the committee asked David to be their Minister of Education and Youth and he accepted the position. Remember how I stated that God opens some doors and closes others? Now we can easily call this one revolving! I had to be sure we heard God's calling and were moving in His will. Rather than be in awe of a long-ago prayer being answered, I could only focus on how a move would negatively impact my life and the network I had enjoyed in my own hometown. How could I just dissolve my Bible study group? I would have to find someone to take over WMU director. I would have to close my gymnastics business. It meant leaving Alabama and moving back to Kentucky. How could we financially do this? Pack up and leave my mom and dad and move again? I decided I was not going to move that gymnastic equipment back to Kentucky! So, what did I do? I got into God's Word and put out a fleece. (A fleece is where you ask God to give you a sign based upon a need being fulfilled. Judges 6)

A friend and I prayed to God and implored of Him that if He really wanted our family to move, then He would have someone approach me to buy my gymnastics business. That may sound like a strange request—but that was MY fleece. And remember, even this sweet, southern, Christian woman was not above selfish prayers to God. However, I really did send out that fleece with all prayerfulness and beseeching the Lord to give us a sign. And, God did! Not only does God have a sense of humor, His timing is perfect. Only a few weeks passed after my prayer when a fellow gymnastics coach in Birmingham, Alabama came to me and asked if I had any equipment that I would be willing to sell him as he was expanding his own gym. I could hardly wait to get home and share with my friend that our fleece prayer had been answered! (We didn't have cell phones or texting back then.)

Now, I do not recommend praying a fleece as Gideon did in Chapter six of the book of Judges. I remember learning in a Bible study one time that we have two tools in place that Gideon, a judge of the Israelites, did not have in place when he prayed his fleece to the Lord. First, we have the complete Word of God. God has assured us that His Word is all we need to be thoroughly equipped as promised to us in 2 Timothy 3: 16-17. Our second advantage over Gideon is that we as Christians have the Holy Spirit. We do not need proof of signs as the Holy Spirit will let us know the Truth. We can have His indwelling presence to guide us. Praying for a fleece is no longer needed. However, it sure didn't hurt anything for me to REALLY search for God's perfect will by appealing to my human frailties. God knew what was best for me and my family. I did not understand it at the time. I had to search for His will through prayer and scripture reading. I began to realize the importance of Colossians 3:16-17.

"<sup>16</sup>Let the word of Christ dwell in you richly in all wisdom; teaching and admonishing one another in psalms and hymns and spiritual songs, singing with grace in your hearts to the Lord. <sup>17</sup> And whatsoever ye do in word or deed, do all in the name of the Lord Jesus, giving thanks to God and the Father by Him." (KJV)

I needed a wisdom that only God could impart. It is hard to look back and see how one moment I could be serving Jesus, and within a matter of hours, I could be so self-serving. I was living in dread, afraid of change and afraid of taking a leap of faith in God. The Word of God teaches us how to live life so that we can have joy in our hearts. To obtain that peace and joy, we need to search the scriptures and write down the truths the Lord reveals to us. What are your desires concerning the Lord? Are you giving your thoughts and deeds to Jesus? At the time, I thought I was. It was much later that I discovered Colossians 3:1-17 was written to give us a guideline for daily living God's plan in our lives. It tells us to put to death all evil desires and greed. I needed the Bible study in my life at that time. After you have read Colossians chapter three, ask God to reveal what it is you need to "put to death." What are the earthly things that keep you from serving the Lord? Is dread or fear inhibiting you from making a needed change in your life? Here are a few lines to write down the answers to the questions. God will bless you as you take the time to reflect and answer the questions above.

_____

_____

_____

_____

_____

_____

Here are a few verses that have helped me in my times of need. The first one helped me in knowing the truth about worldly situations. The second one confirms that Jesus is the only way to salvation and I am to follow His truth and His way.

"And you shall know the truth, and the truth shall make you free." (John 8:32 NKJV)

"I am the way, the truth, and the life. No one comes to the Father except through Me." (John 14:6)

I'll tell you what this reflection did in my life.

Within a couple of months, I had sold all my gymnastics equipment, found a new Director of WMU, and was saying goodbye to all my friends in Christ at First Baptist Oneonta. David and I had prayed for a home to come available since our first visit back to his hometown. Once again, God took care of us and gave us the perfect house for our family. It is amazing what God will do when we follow His truth. We followed His truths as He led us to Alabama after David's stroke. We may have lived with my parents for a little over five years as grown adults who were married and had three girls of our own, but my family thrived because of this. All three girls invited Jesus into their hearts during our time with my loving parents. My girls loved life and God, and they had as much support and love from my parents as they had from David and me. We did not have financial wealth, but we had a wealth of happiness in each other that was not surpassed until our children began to have our grandchildren. Now it was time to follow God's truths again. This time. . .it was back to Kentucky.

What I had prayed for at church camp twenty years earlier was now being fulfilled. (Check # 4) I was so scared and part of me was in disbelief that my prayers of long ago had come true. We became excited about a new ministry and meeting new friends. David was excited about the challenges of growing a youth group. Our girls were not as excited. So that we could help them with the transition, we continued the Bible share time we instituted back in Oneonta. We prayed for our friends back home. We praised God for David's good health. I placed it all in the Lord's hands and depended on friends and family for everything that they offered. My sister-in-law (the one we visited when David had the stroke) came to help me decorate and completely arrange our new home. I depended on David's parents to help me with the girls. As I take this "selfie," I wish that I had been able to read the book by Holley Gerth, <u>You're Going to Be Okay.</u> It had not been written yet. Holley tells us to make the most of all our special moments. She reminds us that God did not create a plan B for our lives.[1] I had to laugh when she penned this truth. And, then she quoted Hebrews 12: 1-2.

---

"Therefore we also, since we are surrounded by so great a cloud of witnesses, let us throw off everything that hinders and the sin which so easily entangles, and let us run with perseverance the race marked out for us. [2]Let us fix our eyes on Jesus, the author and perfecter of our faith. . ."[2]

---

To follow the Truth, we must fix our eyes on Jesus. We must throw off everything that hinders us or leads us into temptation. Are you following the Truth? If not, I pray you will get into a quiet place and realize that we all sin and come short of the glory of the Lord. In God's eyes, all sins are equal. No one has the excuse that they are not good enough to become a Christian! My sins as a Christian are no better or worse than the sins of a non-Christian. The difference is, as a believer, we believe that Jesus is the Son of God and we receive forgiveness when we are faithful to confess those sins. God made a provision for us to forgive us of our sins, all of them. Jesus, God's own Son, went to the cross to die for your sins and my sins that through His resurrection, we might have eternal life. God implores us to go and sin no more. It is up to us to make that 180 degree turn from our sin. What is wonderful, God did not leave us alone. He sent us the Holy Spirit that we might be filled with a comfort and joy and a peace that passes all understanding! Do you have that peace? Are you daily living a joy-filled life? YOU can! Look into your heart. Take that "Selfie" and write down what the Lord reveals to you.

_____

_____

_____

_____

_____

_____

Verses to claim for salvation:

". . .for all have sinned and fall short of the glory of God." (Romans 3:23 NKJV)

"For the wages of sin is death, but the gift of God is eternal life in Christ Jesus our Lord." (Romans 6:23 NKJV)

"For God so loved the world that He gave His only begotten Son, that whosoever believes in Him should not perish but have everlasting life." (John 3:16 NKJV)

Did you ask God to help you make your walk a daily walk? Did you pray and ask Jesus to come into your heart and life? If so, take the opportunity to write below your prayer, and then what it is you must do to follow Jesus in believer's baptism. You will need to talk with a minister of a church to let him know of your decision to follow Christ. If you are rededicating your life, make plans to go forward at your church to make the commitment public. You will receive a peace that passes all understanding and you will have joy! Praise the Lord!

_____

_____

_____

_____

_____

_____

# Chapter Five

# Exodus 2

"For all the law is fulfilled in one word, even in this: 'You shall love your neighbor as yourself.' [15]But if you bite and devour one another, beware lest you be consumed by one another!" (Galatians 5:14-15 NKJV)

Here we are back in David's hometown in Kentucky. We left my hometown in Alabama. This may not seem funny to you, but I have to laugh. You see, there is one thing my husband had always told me when we got married, "I will never live in your hometown, nor will I live in my hometown!" It is difficult, sometimes, to describe God's purpose for us. It is easy to move in His will when our prayers are answered. But, what happens when we follow His will and find a storm ahead? We can begin to doubt we are in God's will.

David began to settle into the role of Minister of Youth and Education. He found willing servants for GA and RA leaders from those church members whom he challenged to get a blessing. I became a GA leader since I had three little GA's already! Besides, no one here knew I had been through the ranks of all the missions groups to the director of WMU. It was time to step aside and enjoy working with the children again. It was such a blessing to see the faces of the children (girls and boys) as we visited the local nursing home. They loved being helpers of everyone they came into contact. Of course, there were numerous other activities we enjoyed which helped us grow to over fifty children on Wednesday nights. After two years, David's youth group had grown to thirty plus. The Lord was blessing David's efforts with great success. For a church of just about one-hundred eighty or so each Sunday, that was pretty good. Actually, it was very good considering that almost half the congregation were senior citizens. David was a hometown boy that most everyone respected.

We soon discovered there were multiple power struggles within the church. Many felt that they could have David influence the pastor to rededicate his efforts to allow the church members to get spending and other problems resolved. The pastor hoped a "hometown" boy would placate the church members and he could continue to enjoy his tenure within the church. Without knowing it, we had moved into the hot coals of church politics. The deacons and pastor looked at David to somehow unify their divided church. For a time, it seemed to be working.

David and I had hoped that the conflict was felt only by us, and that our girls would be spared the heartache and disappointment. They immensely loved God and were such passionate young Christian children. Thus, we tried our best to shield them from the conflict of this church. But, the collision of faith between our daughter who was a young dedicated Christian, and our frustrated church leader would occur. My eldest daughter was a vibrant soul-winning fifth grader when we moved there. She would excitedly approach others and would talk to them of her faith. One night she was sitting beside the church phone in the basement, when it rang. An elderly lady identified herself and called asking for prayers. My daughter was very excited to promise her that she would tell the pastor that we would place her requests on the prayer list. That Wednesday evening, she was beaming as the pastor of our church walked in and she was able to report grown-up prayer requests. She began to tell him of the lady's name and her needs. The pastor cut her off and explained how that lady was always calling about something and he wished she would just quit calling. My mouth dropped, as I was hidden behind the wall and had not been seen. My daughter's face turned red, then hurt and perplexed! She found her tongue first and said that her GA group would pray for her and off she marched. I followed without a word. Now before you start casting stones at the preacher, remember, you without sin, cast the first stone! (John 8: 7 paraphrased) My heart was breaking. It was breaking for the pastor who was preoccupied. It was breaking for my daughter who did not understand his reply. This was our first experience with a church leader, or even a church member, whose heart was not receptive to another member's need. We are all human. In a moment of weakness, even a pastor can fall to selfishness. There is forgiveness! We prayed that night for our daughter, our pastor and our church. Pastors are people too! They need us to pray for them every day. Satan tries very hard to tear down their testimony for Christ. The pastor's human failing helped me to realize how easy it is for us to fall to selfishness. One lesson we learned from this experience was that we were to follow God, not a man of God. So many people leave the church because they follow a mere man rather than God. As I reflect, I heard several meaningful messages from the pastor—even after his mistake that night. It had its effect upon us for as long as we allowed it to. Do not allow others to tear down your joy. If you go back and read this, you will recall we prayed about it that very night. When you are working in the church, do not allow yourself to be hurt by what others may do or say. Pray about it and give it to the Lord. Is it easy? No, but you will keep your joy and love for the Lord and His service if you forgive the flaw in the person who hurt you. Has someone hurt you in God's church? Are you upset with someone in your church? Here are a few lines to write of your hurt and then write a prayer of forgiveness and leave it here on the pages and do not pick it back up. Go to that person and tell them you forgive them. No matter their reaction, love them. If you do love them, it is scriptural that it is like heaping coals of fire on their head. God wants us to forgive them and love them. That is all He asks. May God bless your efforts!

---

---

---

---

---

---

Now that you have forgiven those who would seek to destroy your peace, I would like to address how Jesus' inclusion of children into God's kingdom is of importance to us all. In Jesus' time, children were without rights. They were property, ordered and used however the family and society needed them, or did not. Jesus stated in Matthew 19:14, "Let the little children come to me, and do not hinder them, for the kingdom of heaven belongs to such as these." (NKJV) Please understand the significance of that statement. He admonished His disciples for hindering them. Jesus marked children as something far above a second-class citizen and far greater than the "objects" as they were seen by many in society. He assured us that until they came to the age of accountability, the "kingdom was theirs." Truly, what we learn from Christ is that we should edify, not deter, the faith of a child. If we become child-like in our faith, we will love unconditionally. As adults, we often put conditions on our love—we are selfish. We also must be careful to not lead children astray. We are to set the example of being a disciple for them.

Nurturing our children's innocence and faith would prove difficult, especially as they grew older in the church and in our small town. They were exposed to conflict and judged by many just for being daughters of a Youth and Education Minister. I wanted my girls to have some semblance of normalcy in the midst of almost daily conflicts inside and out of church. Unfortunately, our oldest daughter remembers the manipulation, anger, frustration, and back-stabbing within the church and our church members. I have come to realize churches are no different from other families as they are a family as well. As a family member, we learn the give and take of meeting each other's needs. I think we often forget we must do this in a church family as well. We must be willing to meet the needs of others. We need to pray for each other as we do in our earthly families.

You know, praying without ceasing was what I needed during this time in my life and I was not doing the very thing I needed. Why is that? I was feeling the need to shelter the girls from as much as I could and I probably went overboard in encouraging them to play in sports and be involved in many school activities. This also gave me the opportunity to make new friends outside our church family. Do you find yourself being caught up in all the family activities and leaving little time for church activities? I will have to say that I did multitask somewhat during this time. While doing all these activities, I found a purpose in singing in the church choir, and also writing and being published with an article about youth and seniors working together to serve the Lord. I also published a few devotionals in the SBC choir magazine. At home, we had Bible "share-time" every night before we went to bed and prayed for people we had known in the past and for the ones we were meeting in the present. We tried to do this around 8:00PM every night so that we could have the girls in bed by 8:30. We had them share something good that had happened during the day at school and then share any successes in their activities. Then we would read a scripture and find out what the girls thought about it and how they could apply it to their lives. After that, David would take prayer requests and we would pull a name out of the basket of acquaintances to pray for. Obviously, this is just the format we chose to follow before bedtime. You can decide what is best for your family share time. It is most important that you start a Bible share time. If you already have one, then don't stop it. Your children will grow with the Lord and it will help them to make better decisions as they get older.

As true of all families, we had our ups and downs. That held true for our church family too. God had a purpose in our growing to depend on Him as we struggled through many common church conflicts. God would teach us perseverance and to love others no matter how it seemed they spitefully used us. David and I were in the process of learning forgiveness and humility. I would gain a true understanding of Luke 6: 27-28:

"But I say to you who hear; Love your enemies, do good to those who hate you, [28]bless those who curse you, and pray for those who spitefully use you." (NKJV)

You may have been in a church where a split occurred. You can hear disputes over what color to paint the walls, whether to put pads in the pews, or a group that decides they have all the answers from God and seek to have their way no matter whether it is practical or not. The problem is selfishness! It occurs in our family life. It occurs in our church life. Our church was no different. David and I both have hearts of healing and encouragement. Our advice to the church members was to always pray for each situation and for the pastor. God used this conflict to teach us compassion for even an unlovable church member. We learned that sometimes you just have to hang there, remembering Jesus hung on the cross for us. Words are of no use. We learned to pray without ceasing.

David sought advice from trustworthy individuals who wore hats of leadership in the realm of our Baptist ministry. But the inevitable happened. That small group of individuals won. The pastor resigned. David felt the only way the church could heal was if he also resigned and allowed the church to begin fresh with new ministers. When David told me this news, I was thinking, "No way! Lord! No, not again!" I did not want to move again! And, as God would have it, we did not have to. Isn't it amazing how the Lord takes care of His own? Even those of us who pray amiss, let dust collect on our Bibles, and definitely are not worth the blood our Savior shed on our behalf!

God was rescuing us. At the time, I didn't realize how the Lord was taking care of us. I was just trying to take care of my girls and their needs. We left our church with all grace and dignity. David recommended a pastor for interim. Sometime later, He even recommended the man who would become the pastor of the church. The love we learned for God's people from 1 Corinthians 13:3 took on a new meaning in our hearts. We can give of our time, talents and whole being, but if we have no love for our fellow man, all that work will profit us nothing! We loved **all** the people from our church we were leaving.

The Lord had a plan! The local Christian Church wanted a youth minister and it did not matter to the current pastor that David was a Southern Baptist. They called him to serve as Associate Minister working with the youth, children, and having the opportunity to preach. Again, the Lord blessed David's efforts. It wasn't long before we had about fifty children and youth on a weekly basis. I cannot Praise the Lord enough for the joy and open arms this church congregation gave us during this time of transition. Our ministry at the Christian church was a very good one and the girls enjoyed going on various trips with the youth snow skiing or canoeing in Indiana or roughing the water rapids in Kentucky and Tennessee. The Lord blessed us during the five years of our service there. However, we all began to yearn to return to the Baptist church. The new pastor of the Baptist church wanted David to help in ministries and return to the church where all of us still had our membership. By this time, my oldest daughter had graduated. When you read the next chapter, you will discover how I tried to handle the teen years. When I take that "selfie," I cannot give myself a pat on the back. I feel as if I failed miserably in some aspects but did well in others. When I allowed the Lord to lead me, of course, those were the good times. However, I allowed my pride and wanting to be a part of the "group" cause me much anguish. I did not serve the Lord while at the Christian church other than as a Sunday school teacher. I did not allow the Lord to lead me as I had back in Alabama. I had become self-seeking. I placed more interest in my earthly friends than I did in walking in the Spirit. It had taken several years for this to occur. I did not realize what was happening. It reminds me of the struggle Paul wrote about in Romans 7:19-20.

19"For the good that I will to do, I do not do; but the evil I will not to do, that I practice. 20Now if I do what I will not to do, it is no longer I who do it, but sin that dwells in me."

I was **not** doing what I knew to do! Dust was gathering on my Bible! I was not learning any new scriptures. I would go by my Bible and say to myself, "I'll stop and read a scripture when I finish doing what I am doing." You guessed it, it never happened! Paul penned it perfectly. I knew to study and read God's Word. I wanted to. I just did not do it! Are you caught in this trap? Are you practicing worldly activities you know you shouldn't? Here are a few lines for confession and then make a plan to correct what you should do.

_____

_____

_____

_____

_____

_____

# Chapter Six

# The Teen (10) Plagues

1. Sweet girls going through puberty

2. Bickering

3. Lies

4. Drugs & Alcohol

5. Family financing

6. Small town alliances

7. Peer Pressure

8. Lost innocence/faith

9. Expectations of the Preacher's kids

10. The loss of "family share time"

"Stand fast therefore in the liberty by which Christ has made us free, and do not be entangled again with a yoke of bondage." (Galatians 5: 1 NKJV)

I was chasing after my youngest child as fast as I could with a flip flop extended as if I was going to do real damage. She was screaming something about the fact that she was innocent! Since I had lost the race, I stopped and started laughing in hysterics. I can't even remember why I was so angry with her. To this day, we laugh over the comical sight of me chasing after my first grader with a flip flop in hand. I'm sure she needed discipline—I just was going about it in the wrong way. Their father would bark, "Young lady!" or, call them by their three birth names, and they would promptly freeze. They wanted to flee from their fathers' discipline. Not because he did them any bodily harm, but because he made them stop and answer many questions about the choices they were making. He made them accountable. This accountability would serve each of them well as they became independent. At the time, they dreaded those talks.

What was happening to my sweet little girls that told their mommy everything and would not dream of talking back? It is called puberty! I remember one night when one of the girls got caught slipping back into the house with a friend. After curfew, one of our daughter's and her friend secretly left the house. David heard them and went downstairs to wait in our daughter's room for their return. Since it was past their curfew, I was sound asleep. Not their father. When they sneaked back into the house, they found David lying in their bed. He sat up and told both girls that they would have to stand at the end of the bed and watch him sleep! The friend started to protest, but David explained she had been a willing participant in the rule breaking, hadn't she? She agreed that she had. Then, he concluded it was only fair she serve in the consequences of those actions. Thirty minutes later, he asked them to tell him why curfews were needed. They gave all the standard answers including for their own protection. They learned a valuable lesson that night. That was the last time **that** friend tried to sneak out of the house with our daughter.

Back then, David and I had more arguments than I could count about raising our three teenage daughters'. I was a "softie." He held the girls accountable. Then, how could we possibly argue, and on a daily basis? I wasn't really listening to my husband, nor was I listening to my daughters, much less God! I poured myself into church programs, teaching gymnastics to cheerleaders and running three girls to their respective events. Sounds good doesn't it? I thought I had it all together and was serving the Lord. Or, was I just pretending I was righteous? Only a few short years before, I really was serving my Lord. I had allowed my selfish ways to creep back into my life and the devil had placed blinders on my eyes and heart. I did not see this happening! I was too busy running my two eldest daughters to cheer in ballgames and my youngest daughter to track events and basketball games. I had stopped depending on the Lord and was trying to raise three girls without His help and guidance. The writer of Hebrews wanted us to have a picture of the discipline of God so that we could in turn learn to discipline our own children. He cross-referenced the passage from Revelation 3:19 where it proclaims,

"My son, do not despise the chastening of the Lord,

Nor be discouraged when you are rebuked by Him:

For whom the Lord loves He chastens,

And scourges every son whom He receives."

We all need boundaries. Adam and Eve were given boundaries in the Garden of Eden. The boundaries that David and I had been so successful at keeping when the girls were younger came to a dramatic head as the girls hit puberty. As stated before, no one warned me about puberty! I did not have siblings as I was growing up because my only sister was thirteen years older. I did not realize my innocent girls could become masters of deception. It seemed we were visited by the ten plagues of Israel! Remember, the Israelites had to endure most of those plagues with the Egyptians. As a family, we must learn to endure all our problems together. We must learn to do so in prayer and that was what I was neglecting to do. Are you in prayer over your teens or someone else you love who has teens? When I took the "selfie" here, I learned how important it is to stay in prayer for our children and grandchildren. I do so daily.

Like most church goers, we were serving God and going to church with our three girls every time the doors opened. At some point, our good attendance was supposed to make us perfect, or at least Godly, right? How could it? I was becoming very self-centered as were the girls. We were busy with worldly activities and giving very little time to the Lord. David was extremely busy with seminary courses and working with youth. I was trying hard to keep three preteens happy. Like I said before, David and I managed to argue over my lack of discipline and communication on a daily basis. During this time of pouring myself into the **world**, and a little time into the Bible, I was reminded through a Bible study one day that I needed to be more Christ-like. My Bible study class brought the revelation, yet again, that I needed a closer walk with the Lord. My husband and I should have been praying about our relationship to each other and to the Lord. Because I was so busy with worldly activities, I neglected to do that which I knew to do. Like so many parents, I became a taxi service running children to either cheer at a game or actually play in a game. The two elder daughters became cheerleaders while their younger sister chose the sports of basketball and track. During the eldest daughter's senior year, the schedule for cheering and games did not coincide very often. It was very hard to keep up with their demands. I was not being a consistent disciplinarian. This fact led to the joy of Jesus being stripped from our lives.

There were other plagues that would strip us of our joy. There were financial boundaries. On such a modest income, we had to watch our spending. My oldest demanded the best brand name clothes possible. Needless to say, our pocketbooks did not match her requests! There were several arguments between my husband and myself regarding the family budget. David tried to put the reins on spending. It seemed impossible for me to say no—to either side! Occasionally, the eldest would get the new pair of jeans, and at times, her sisters would receive the hand-me-downs from their sister. We were providing the needs as best we could. I did not understand how the lack of extra money had such a profound effect upon our eldest daughter until just recently. I overheard her sharing with a friend how she grew up in Alabama with a loving family who tried to give her sisters and herself their wants; but more often than not, it was only the needs that were met. She was sharing about the day I sent her to school picture day in a trendy sweater that had someone else's initials on it. My daughter pulls out a picture of a toothless first grade girl wearing a sweater that had SFG centered perfectly on the white sweater. My daughter's initials are LMW! The friend laughed aloud. My daughter told her she had verifiable proof because it was picture day in Alabama. Those school pictures that go into the yearbook are the ones we look at twenty years later! I suppose, upon reflection, it did have an effect upon my oldest child. In Kentucky, we were saving money for seminary courses. There were many times my girls would want something their friends had and we just could not give it to them. We gave them plenty of love, but the world has a way of making kids think you don't love them unless you give, give, and give until you bleed! If you have children, I'm sure you can identify. Even today, children want to be able to wear what their friends wear to school. My eldest daughter told me she feels the need to spend large amounts of money on her four children. She showers them with love and waits on each of them endlessly, but she still feels the need to give them the things that she went without. She is very sharing and caring and donates a large amount of time and money to many charities. She recently shared that although she still struggles to maintain the balance of giving into material possessions, she has begun to accept that God has more than blessed their needs and she gains blessings in helping others in need.

I'm sure some of you can identify with trying to make ends meet and giving your children "some" of their wants. It can be a daily struggle. But, you can have joy and be satisfied when you understand the need for a budget and wise spending. On the other spectrum, there are those of you who have the money to give much to your children. Be careful. They must be taught a work ethic from age two. I'm serious! Children, who have everything given to them without a value system in place, will likely be set up for failure, and not necessarily financial failure. There are many young people who are so used to having their parents pay for their way that they cannot survive without the continued aid. Their "wants" give way to the "needs." Eventually, they need more and more to satisfy their wants. Credit cards become maxed out and their debt grows out of hand. This cycle exists outside the Holy Spirit and outside God's plan for us to serve others.

I will also address the parent who does teach their children spiritual values and, yet, the child neglects to follow those values. Those parents need our prayer support as they often feel that, somehow, it was their fault their child became enamored by the ways of the world, even to the point of self-destruction. Everyone is accountable for their own actions, especially children who have been raised in the Word and know God's expectations of them. These children are better equipped than non-believers. Unfortunately, it does not keep them from falling hard in this harsh provocative world. Many a child has lost their innocence due to their own selfish desires—not what their parents taught or didn't teach. Keep praying for the children who have been led astray. God gives us a great promise in Ephesians 6:2-3. Don't give up on your teens—I didn't. I did many things wrong during this time in my life, but I also did one thing right. I prayed for my girls.

Naturally, in our home, there were boundaries against drugs and sex. David and I set clear boundaries about these lifestyle choices. We expected the girls to stay away from these. All young adults are exposed to peer-pressure and the desire to be accepted. Sometimes acceptance is driven by "exploration" and that exploration can become sin. God challenges all to flee from a life of sexual immorality, impurity, lust, evil desires and greed. (Found in Colossians 3:5-10) God gives countless examples in the Old and New Testament as to the consequences of living in these sins. We taught the girls right from wrong. David and I taught the girls about sexual immorality and that God has a perfect mate for each person that He creates. We told them to wait until God's intended mate was brought into their lives before giving way to sex. I don't remember reading specific scriptures to them personally. I wish I could say that I did so to prove our case through the Word of God. I wish I had discussed these scriptures to them time and again during those teenage years. My downfall was that I was not sharing God's stories with my girls to equip them to stand against those worldly temptations. Yes, they did hear these scriptures in their father's youth group studies, but I was not rein-forcing and helping them understand the bible scriptures. There are so many good Bible stories you can share with your teen. During our Bible share times, we were so proud of the girls when they shared successes they related against falling into temptations. Some of these stories were later communicated when they revealed failures and learned to depend on God's love and forgiveness. However, when our eldest was a junior in high school, our Bible share time came under attack by Satan and the influences of the world. It wasn't long before we rarely met for praying together.

More plagues involved bickering, manipulation and lies. Our girls took every advantage they could, pitting their unsuspecting mother against their father at every turn. I have a memory of claiming that I know our daughters would not lie to me! I laugh about this now and how naïve I was. At any rate, fleeing from the sin of lying was also my own biggest prayer as I found myself lying to David to keep the girls from getting into trouble. When I took this "selfie" I had to wonder what in the world I was thinking! I had to offer up my own weaknesses and admit that my "protecting" my girls with lies of my own, was not actually protecting them at all. I was enabling lies and deception. It caused a tremendous lack of respect from my husband at the time. As I stated before, I definitely was not the disciplinarian in our family. But what was worse, I thought David's punishment was too harsh and I often tried to get the girl's sentences reduced. I was inadvertently not supporting my husband. I would later explain to the girls how I was wrong in doing this and ask for their forgiveness. I had to ask forgiveness from David. I pray you do not allow such behavior to happen in your marriage or family. How did I allow myself to be so deceived? It is called selfishness! I thought what I was doing was best. I was not reading my Bible during this time. I was not praying very often and did not have a daily walk with the Lord. I just wanted to freeze my children, like fish, at age thirteen and thaw them out at age twenty-one! LOL

Of course, not all of the teen years were awful. The truth is that we all learn through making our own decisions, good or bad, and using the outcome to determine our next decisions. We forget to go to God's word for our EVERY decision and let Him lead us. It is human temptation to abandon God's plan and try to fulfill our own selfish desires. Our teens are no different than us—just younger and less wise in some cases. We must continue loving them unconditionally and providing them with spiritual revelations to equip them opposite from what the world is telling them.

There were times our girls would share with us how they wanted to help others in need. At every Thanksgiving and Christmas season, we gave food, clothing and gifts to those with need. There was one such occasion that we were given a name of a family where the father had lost his job and they would not be able to give their children Christmas. We were not in great financial shape ourselves, but we sacrificed to help someone else. We traveled to this home that was much larger than ours and had new bicycles out front and a four wheeler. We knocked on the door and were invited into a home with a huge screen TV (we had never seen one that big) and a boy was playing a video game on the TV. Needless to say, our girls were hurt over us taking food, clothing and games to this family. We explained to them that they probably got on the Christmas angel list because their father lost his job and they would not have Christmas otherwise. But, it did leave a bitter taste in our eldest daughters' heart and a hurtful knowledge as we drove away, knowing that these people had so much more than our own girls. Our girls had old bicycles, no "four wheeler," no big screen TV and no video games! We were determined to not let that scenario happen again so we screened our Christmas angels from then on.

As our girls continued to draw further and further from us, they also withdrew from the Christian sanctuary we had created—Family share time. I mentioned this previously and the importance they felt it held in our lives. My girls remember very well, running down the stairs to the family room and sitting around as we would read Scripture, discuss how it related to our daily experiences, and pray together as a family. It was also where we challenged one another to think of others and what we could be as the body of Christ. Sadly, as teens, it became "boring," "no longer needed," and, "just for kids." Or, at least that is what our children were saying at the time. Perhaps David and I allowed our long work days to play a part as well. If you ask the girls about their regrets from their adolescent years, they name giving up Family Share Time. It was indeed their sanctuary and that which was most needed to navigate them through the most challenging of years. I allowed a Godly principle to stop. I was being deceived. What is worse—I did not even recognize the fact.

However, I must state we were all kids once. We certainly did not always want our parents to know what we did and who it was with.

There were times we told those "little white lies" to keep from being grounded. However, sin has a way of clouding our judgment to the point we claim, "I don't care." Have you heard your teenager make this statement? This is really a cry to have clear boundaries. In thirty-eight years of parenting and grand-parenting, I've heard them all. While our girls were teens—I just didn't know it! Statements like, "Just get off my case!" or "Leave me alone!" These are all teenage cries for needing boundaries and wanting to understand something that they do not understand. For some reason, I kept thinking that things would get better. How could they? I was not listening to my children's cry for help and I was too busy with my own self-fulfilling needs to realize this. Sometimes it takes a catastrophic event to humble you and have you re-evaluate your dependence upon the Lord. I will address this in the next chapter.

Living in a small town has its advantages and disadvantages. My Christian witness would be somewhat similar to many of the reality TV shows people love to watch. It is human nature to enjoy seeing others struggle with their challenges and secretly take joy in their failures. Our family endured all of our challenges not unlike your family. While "it takes a village" is commonly cited in a good light, the village can quickly turn against one. The girls would be befriended, cherished, and praised, and at the same time, threatened, manipulated, and detested by the same people. The action of any 'normal' teenager was quickly judged. Facebook and other media have made this judge-ment a daily occurrence in our society. Back then, the telephone was the major form of communication. An example of this came when a lady from church called me to let me know what my child had supposedly done at a party. Upon research, my child was partly guilty of the rumor. Maybe she never found out her daughter was guilty as well. I find that some people are very quick to point out the flaws you have, but do not take a "selfie" themselves. Jesus addressed this in Matthew 7: 1-6. If you have not read it, please do. Jesus knew we would want to judge others failures. It makes us feel better about our own failures. We are to stay in prayer and lift others up, not put them down. This fact will give us true joy in our hearts. The joy that comes from selfish desires only last a short while. It is like a drug, you feel good for a short time and then you need another fix. I knew a lady in church that could not wait until she could tell another 'juicy' gossip tidbit to her circle of friends. It did not matter if it hurt others. She thrived on the negative attitudes that resulted. She was blinded by an evil spirit. I'm sure you know some of those people as well. Pray for them that their eyes would be opened and that they too will find true joy in following Jesus.

There also can be the plague of small town alliances that can cripple your joy as well. It wasn't long after we moved back to Kentucky, that our two eldest girls would experience how alliances could hurt. Our eldest felt the most heartache from the "queen bee" syndrome. Girls can be very cruel to each other during the pre-teen and teen years. If you have young teens, you are well aware of the persecution and bullying that can occur for many various reasons. My girls would overcome the persecution through prayer and discussion of the situations. It was not without hurt and some tears, but as they grew they learned valuable life lessons. They both would become stronger adults. These persecutions can also happen in the adult years to individuals. Do you know someone it has happened to? Yes, even Jesus was persecuted and nailed to a cross because of rumors and alliances of the Sadducees and Pharisees. Our family lived through these persecutions and became stronger. You can do the same—no matter your circumstances. It takes praying without ceasing to live through life's problems. (1 Thessalonians 5:17)

You might ask, "How can two dedicated individuals who love the Lord, experience such pain and suffering?" You cannot point fingers without three pointing back at you. The teen "plague" years are hard on any family. But, there is so much joy in those years, that it out-weighs the negative. There is no way to say if we had just done this, this would not have happened. There are those times that the Lord allows us to go through the consequences of our sin to strengthen us. Is life fair or perfect? No! We can get through all our trials by calling upon the name of Jesus to carry us through. I would find myself doing this over and over. Again, I want to point out that your teens will make their decisions. We would love to make their decisions for them, but that in itself is not healthy. Teens never grow up to become adults when you "bail" them out of their self-made circumstances. They must be allowed to live with their own consequences no matter the price. I know—it is tough. I'm reminded of a teen whose parents had a DUI taken away through their influence. Several months later, they were faced with their teen going to jail because he drove drunk a second time and a life was taken. We are told in Proverbs to train up a child in the way they should go. We are to train. Then, we are to commit to God that training and give them to the Lord. It is penned here again to allow you to see how easy it is for all of us to neglect to do those things we know to do. Paul in Romans 7:19 summed it up perfectly, "[19] For the good that I will to do, I do not do; but the evil I will not to do, that I practice." Taking this "selfie" has been very challenging. Again, I pray you never have to go through the deserts to get to the Promised Land. However, I know that most of you have similar trials. If I could leave you with any advice on how to overcome the "Teen Plagues" it would be to have you implement Bible Share Time each and every night as your children are growing. Then, don't allow anything to stop you!

I do have the joy of remembering each of our girls sitting down with us after college and giving us the "you actually knew what I needed back in the day" speeches and sharing how they now understood as if some great light-bulb had come on in their brains. They now knew we loved them and they shared the great revelation with us that they loved us too! We have to chuckle over our daughters realizations! We have been so blessed with our children and our grandchildren. David and I pray daily for our grandchildren to make wise decisions that will be pleasing to the Lord. We also have others praying for our family. If you haven't done this, please get some great prayer warriors to pray for your family daily. This is a necessity in today's world!

Those of you who have already lived through the teenage years with your children—may God bless you! Those of you who will endure living through the teenage years with your children—may God bless you! Engage in activities that will keep your family involved together. Make sure that the majority of those activities are Christ-centered and your joy will abound. We had many a joyous time hiking and camping on very little money. We always had devotions and shared about God's beauty. We also traveled to visit relatives and instilled in them the value of family. I believe we must be consistent in raising our children from the first to the last. You may be finding consistency in your life problematic. You will want to have a time of reflection to find what needs to be done to become more consistent daily. This action will facilitate better communication with your family. You should make the reflection with the help of God's guidance. In Proverbs 3:6 we are to put God first in everything we do and He will direct and crown our efforts with success. (Paraphrased) The key is to communicate. We must talk to God and we must talk to our loved ones.

For those of You who do not have children, contact a friend to pray for and assist in nurturing their children, and may God bless your efforts. As Christians, we all want to have perfectly normal children who are smart and do all the right things and say all the right things. Anything different can make us feel like we are failures as parents and that somehow we are not living up to God's standards. You need to remember that children must make their own decisions and live with those decisions. You can guide, but they ultimately choose their destiny. It is much easier to guide if your children are friends with other children who have the same values as you. You may want to write down how you can witness and lead your own children and their friends to participate in Godly activities. Involving your children in church activities will keep them grounded in the Word and equip them with the value of prayer and Bible study. Make a list of activities that you can get your children involved that has little if any financial cost.

_____

_____

_____

_____

_____

_____

Another problem with raising our young children today is what they see on TV and on video games. I used to watch a multitude of worthless things on TV. How about you? How about your children? Like most Christian parents, we did not want our children subjected to the language, sex and demeaning that most TV shows and movies allowed. It is even harder now as there are all the social media sites that children can sometimes gain access without parental knowledge. You can place firewalls and other stops to hopefully stop them. However, there are some children that can get around whatever you place on their devices. I've known of children going to porn sites and their parents did not have a clue what they were doing until the FBI knocked on their door. Boy, were they shocked! Psalm 119: 37 addresses the issue. It tells us to turn our eyes away from looking at worthless things. The Psalmist then adds that we should be revived in God's ways. We need to pray this prayer daily. God will take away the need to watch worthless things on TV, You Tube, or any other printed material. Write your prayer to God and make a plan of how to keep worthless things out of your life.

_____

_____

_____

_____

_____

_____

# Chapter Seven

# The Prodigal Child

"...for this my son was dead and is alive again; he was lost and is found.' And they began to be merry." (Luke 15:24 NKJV)

"**W**hat can you learn from this situation?" my husband would ask our daughters when they had made a mistake and needed to learn a life lesson. The father in the prodigal story probably thought about asking a similar question after the son returned. I began to ask myself this question as I took a deeper look into the lessons I could learn.

Throughout the New Testament, the Gospel message is one of love which seeks lost things. Hey, I get it, David and I have had many anguished moments over me losing the keys, my wallet, the phone, my passport. . .you get the picture. Naturally, the finding or recovery of lost human souls is more important. In Luke 15:1-32, Jesus illustrates three 'lost and found' parables—better known, the prodigal (lost) son. This parable has many applications to life's experiences.

I'm going to provide you with examples from my childhood and my middle daughter's life experiences to enable you to understand that even a child of God can find themselves "lost" in worldly conflicts and that God is faithful to show us a way to find that which was lost.

Our middle daughter was given a bountiful supply of gifts by God—a kind, carefree, artistic, eager to please child. She freely gave her laughter and praise, excited by what she could do for others. She was a cheerleader, painted, wrote poetry and loved all people. She asked Jesus into her life at a young age. The teenage years can be hard on our children—especially a preacher's kid! Our compassionate daughter began to try to please the wrong people. Like the younger son in Jesus' parable, she became tired of school and all the petty popularity contests, mediating family disputes, and tending to what was expected of her as a preacher's daughter.

She became wearied with her scheduled school activities and encouraging others when she herself needed more encouragement. Her older sister had entered college and left her the "big sister" to her younger sibling. We thought we had a happy teenager who very rarely gave us any trouble. She never talked back like her two siblings and she met her curfews. She was so sweet and caring and wanted to please everyone, so it seemed. She was a master at keeping her feelings hidden. The first warning sign that all was not as it seemed came when she announced she wasn't going out for cheerleader as she needed to concentrate on her studies. I did not realize this as a warning. Her new found friends seemed really nice and they went to many events together. I did not have a clue that they would go to one of the friends' home after school or on weekends to smoke marijuana. As her mother, many would have thought I would have recognized her unhappiness. I did not. Like the prodigal son, she did not anticipate her friends would leave her. She fell into depression battling several issues. I relate this story to help you understand that you can live and love your own flesh and blood and not really know what they feel when there is a breakdown in communication. My eldest daughter often asked me to sit down and discuss feelings and needs and wants with her. That was her personality—getting it all out on the table. Our middle child was a typical middle child, who **never asked** for anything. I had neglected to properly communicate with our middle child. As I look back, I could have claimed I didn't have time because I was teaching middle school full-time and grading papers and numerous other life responsibilities. This does not excuse the fact that I neglected to discuss her feelings and actions. How can children be led in the right path unless you **make the time** to nurture and communicate? There was no consistency on my behalf. I held to the belief everything would turn out okay.

Like the father in the prodigal story, I woke up to a very confused and scared child. David had warned me that my lack of communication was hurting family relationships. I resolved to "fix" the problem but did not pray about it. Instead, I filled my life with church work and friends of my own. I pretended that all was okay until one day our high school counselor called to let us know our beautiful daughter needed our help. Desperate for a future, she volunteered her admittance into a recovery facility to get the help she needed. After her initial treatment, we were so happy to have her come home. Her younger sister was ecstatic to have her sweet sister return! We set up some family counseling sessions to enable all of us to communicate our feelings and thoughts. I continued to have problems with this area of my life. I thought I was communicating. I did not realize that there was so much unsaid.

Our family and friends were praising the Lord for our child's return. Our daughter's peers did not. They mercilessly scoffed and spread rumors. They enjoyed taunting, rather than welcoming her home. But God's promise is to return that which is lost. Realizing that we were "at a cross-road" and that she could not continue facing the unwelcoming small-town gossips, we began to discuss our options as a family. After months of prayer and evaluation, we did what no parent would ever want to do. There was a consensus within our family that Our daughter needed a fresh start. It was the most grueling decision a mother and father could ever make. Our hearts were breaking! Again, I put out that prayer fleece and prayed that God direct her path, keep her well and grow her into what He wanted her to be. She evaluated the choices. She considered living with aunts in Alabama, Ohio or with a missionary friend in Kenya, Africa. Praying these prayers, we surrendered custody of her to David's eldest sister and our precious daughter left her loving family for a loving caring aunt in Ohio. There, she would not need to conform or suffer from small town focus and attention. She would have the chance to begin anew and walk with God to get through the challenges ahead. She began this journey in the middle of her junior year in high school. There is a bible verse that gave David and me a peace about what we knew we must do. (Romans 12:2 NKJV) "And do not be conformed to this world, but be transformed by the renewing of your mind, that you may prove what is that good and acceptable and perfect will of God." Our sweet little girl was renewing her mind and spirit without the hindrance's she had left behind. I cried with joy in my heart that day because I knew the Lord would bless her. She excelled in her studies. She excelled in her art. She made new friends that accepted her for the beautiful caring person they came to know. She was so far away, but we kept up with her successes, and the distance was an enormous gift because none of the influences of our small town could reach her through the miles.

I pray you never have to go through something like this with one of your own children. It is devastating! You feel so helpless! At first, I felt such a failure as a mom. The Lord helped me to realize that I was being a caring mom to be willing to allow Him to nurture our daughter through her aunt. Words cannot describe the void we felt with our middle child out of our home. We made it through that time with the help of the Lord and the great reports we received from her aunt. We visited every chance we could. We even got to help her get ready for prom and other events that parents love to share with their children. We rejoiced with her as she walked the aisle toward graduation with honors. Not only that, but four years later, we were filled with rejoicing as she graduated Cum Laude from the University of Louisville. Our prodigal child had been found! Praise God He carried us through the challenges we faced during this time. Today, our middle child is happily married and has one son—our seventh grandchild. She and her husband are successful in their chosen professions. They too struggle with schedules of raising their four year old. Within his first year of life, he had fifteen different doctors who saw him for Neurofibromatosis, Type 1 (NF1). We praise God daily that he is tumor free thus far. We continue to pray for a cure. The disorder often developmentally delays physical, intellectual and emotional growth. We again praise God that our grandson has a mild case compared to so many who struggle to lead normal childhood lives. Several of you reading this may identify with the struggle of living with a special needs child. It is by the grace of God that you can meet each new day with joy and understanding. There is one piece of advice my daughter would want me to share with you. Become your child's biggest advocate by joining a parent group in whatever special needs area your child is involved. You will meet others who go through the same struggles you do. As I look at my "selfie," I realized that the reason I could go through these trials with my children were two-fold. I had a support group of friends within the church and I had a wonderful supportive husband who hugged me, loved me, and made sure I knew everything would work out for the best. I am still learning from this situation.

It is appropriate here to look within yourself and do some per-sonal reflection as I have done. You are not always what you think you are. You are not always what others describe you to be. As a child of God, you are much more than you can possibly imagine. Take a moment and let that sink in! You are what you think, and believe in your heart. If you think positive thoughts, then you are more positive than negative. You enjoy life and others see goodness, gentleness, and kindness in your life. If you focus on being a child of God, of having a positive faith, you live with the greatest strength imaginable. What will you do with that strength? My weaknesses become strength when I give them to the Lord. The problem is this. I am still learning to give my problem of communicating with others to the Lord. Please allow me to explain. I must go back to a time in my childhood that has unpleasant memories. It is not an occasion I like to talk about because it brings sad remembrances of my mother when she was diagnosed with schizophrenia. Before she was diagnosed, she heard voices telling her awful things. She would have me play inside a spacious cabinet to protect me from those voices she feared. As a four year old, that protection gave me a very creative mind. I played for what seemed like hours inside that cabinet and never realized my mother's problem. Inside my small, innocent mind, I created a fun and beautiful world. One that I often choose to believe existed as reality. I learned to be happy in my own thoughts and I didn't necessarily need to communicate with others to function. I now realize those unknowing circumstances took its toll on me in ways I am still dealing with today. Communicating with others is not an easy task for me. Of course, when my father realized her sickness, he sought treatment for my mother. Doctors treated her with shock therapy and medicine that countered her paranoia and resolved the voices. Most people did not know of my mothers' battle with those demons as she was one of the most giving and unselfish individuals that I have ever known. If I had told people my mother battled such, they would not have believed me. She realized that a mind must have more than medication to stabilize and nurture itself. I grew up watching her read the Bible and, on occasion, she read aloud to me as I sat at her feet. I think back to that little girl playing in that cupboard and I thank the Lord that she did read the Bible to me. She gave me a love for God's word and like her, I can experience daily joy.

We have watched our middle daughter become the beautiful vibrant young wife and mother that she is today. She shines! During the most challenging life events I have experienced, God has been and continues to be that shining light. I live in this knowledge, but, like some of you, struggle daily to put feet into action. I still find myself blocking out situations that I do not want to deal with. It is hard for me to recall events of the past and I typically get them out of order. I depend on God and my husband to help me as I work on communicating. If there is one thing you can learn from the last two chapters, I hope it is that you need a support group to help you resolve issues and grow in the Lord. Contact a sister, brother, or any other relative who can pledge support as you raise your children. When dealing with the teen years, spending quality time with them helps your children know the unconditional love that God wants all of us to experience. I realize the hectic schedule of this world has made us think it is impossible to spend time with our loved ones. We selfishly allow that. But wasn't that why God had Jesus come to earth? Not only did He provide a way for our salvation, but He provided a way for us to "go and make disciples." Read Matthew 28:16 and realize God has commanded us to spend time with others, discipling. We show

His love when we share with others through discipleship. Now take a few moments and make a plan to gather contacts to enable you to grow and make disciples. Who do you know? Make a list of those who can pledge support to pray for your family. Then, write down the activities that can draw you closer as a family. Make a plan!

_____

_____

_____

_____

_____

_____

## Chapter Eight

# Ye, Who Are Weary

"Come to me, all you who are weary and burdened, and I will give you rest." (Matthew 11:28 NIV)

All parents need to claim this verse during the teen plague years. David and I needed rest from three very active and somewhat rebellious teens. Now don't get me wrong, they were also very sweet, loving and caring. They would take up for anyone they counted as their friend or those who were considered less privileged and ridiculed. They loved and adored their grandparents and helped them continuously. They were human. They were growing up in a "me" generation and they were more self-centered than Christ-centered. They were not mature enough in their Christian walks to make wise decisions based on Christ-like values. You know, there are great men and women of the Bible that raised their children to love the Lord. We can read of examples where some children followed the Lord and of others who fell away from following God because of their wrong decisions. I praise the Lord that even though our daughters each had their hours of darkness, they made decisions that brought them back to the Cross. It could be possible you are one of those teens reading this book. You need to claim Ephesians 6:2-3:

> "'Honor your father and mother,' which is the first commandment with promise: ³"that it may be well with you and you may live long on the earth."

Did you know this is a promise for you? You may have made decisions that you feel are so bad you can never return to a better life. Through Jesus, all things are possible! He can clean you up and give you hope. He can give you a peace that passes all understanding! You need to fall on your knees and ask Him to forgive you and then get up and walk in a new life. Share with your parents what you have done. Find other Christians to rejoice with. My eldest daughter wanted me to share her story with you to see that even when it seems all odds are against you, depending on Jesus can get you through your trials.

My eldest daughter fell in love with a young man during her first semester in college. She thought he was "the one." In her young, inexperienced mind, she thought they shared similar interests, friends and goals. They continued dating through her freshman and sophomore years of college. During the summer between her sophomore and junior year, she discovered, and yet refused to believe, that she was pregnant. She convinced herself that she had salmonella poisoning when she threw up relentlessly after making cupcakes with her little cousins. She was back on campus when we got the call she needed to share with us about her condition. David and I were devastated. As we silently drove to meet her, we prayed for God to give us guidance on what to say to our child who needed our support. David and I spent several hours grieving with her over the young man whom she had loved. He had now abandoned her and she didn't even know where he was. His parents had withdrawn him from the school and placed him into another school in another state. He had been on soccer scholarship and she found out from his friends what had been done. We cried together and prayed together for God's guidance. We discussed the option of giving up the baby for adoption to some couple who wanted one but could not conceive. Our daughter knew, without hesitation, that she would rather go it alone, with our help of course, than give up a baby God had given her. We trusted God that He would be with her and that His child would be special. She went back to her room that night and wrote a sign to place over her bed. "Trust in the Lord with all your heart and lean not unto your own understanding." (Proverbs 3:5 NKJV) With this verse, she found peace. I did not know about this sign until I began writing this book. Our daughters' roommates became stronger Christians because they witnessed the determination she had against all odds. She didn't understand why the baby's father had left her alone. She simply trusted God to work it all out. She shared with us that she remembered seeing an angel when she was six years of age. She knew that angel was with her and that the angel and God would get her through this time. She knew that David and I loved and supported her and that she did not ever have to look back at the decision to raise her child with anything but joy.

What would follow would be weeks of standing firm and not conforming to him and his family's requests or months of silence. She didn't know where the father was living and he did not call. She grieved over losing her babies' father. She didn't know whether he would come back to be a part of the baby's life. She didn't know if he had abandoned just her or if he had abandoned his baby forever. Her roommates consoled and stood firm to help her. She waited tables to raise money for herself and her unborn son to live on. It was not easy. But the Lord was with her every step. She had an army of people in the delivery room to support and love her. The nurses could not believe all the people who came to support her. She gave birth to our grandson between the fall and spring semester break. For the next semester, she drove one-hundred fifty miles per day three days per week. She returned to live in the university town at the beginning of her senior year. While our daughter and grandson lived with us we all had so much fun taking turns walking and singing to a grandson who had the colic. The music we played was our oldies from the 50's and 60's during 1998. Those were precious times.

One of our eldest daughter's greatest successes is not conforming to the world and its demands. When she is against a wall, she perseveres. When she is weak, she finds strength in God, rather than short-sighted dependence on society. What happens when we give up ourselves, when we conform to God's plan, rather than the world? For our daughter, it meant bringing an amazing young man into this world. For, without following God's plan, he would likely not have been born. It meant trusting in God to raise him, to teach him important lessons. It meant that our daughter would embrace hard work, determination, and lean on God and family to get through the most difficult times. It meant continuing education—earning a Master's Degree—to improve her son's quality of life. And, it meant forgiveness. She would learn to love and forgive the very person who abandoned her and their unborn child, so that her son could learn love and forgiveness and forge a relationship with his father. There are few examples of forgiveness like the forgiveness that our daughter gave to the father and his parents.

When our grandson was eleven months old, the father finally asked to see his son. We praised God as we had prayed for this. His parents, realizing that they had a grandson reached out to her and asked to see him.  God had allowed our daughter a peace and calm toward his parents that barred any anger or resentment she could have felt toward them. David and I had also forgiven their moment of weakness and were jubilant over their decision to give our grandson two sets of loving grandparents. Children need a loving father, even if he is not in their immediate life. They need to know they were not abandoned. Without hesitation, she allowed them into the life and that of her sweet, talking, running eleven month-old boy who was named after my father. Every person who meets my oldest grandson loves him instantly. My daughter claims that God created him to do great things. He does great things every day in our minds. He is a natural athlete and whatever sport he chooses to play, he has gifted ability. He was also gifted academically and socially. People gravitate toward his personality. God's presence in our daughter's and her son's life has been the deciding difference in the joy and happiness that they have experienced out of the uncertainty they once faced. My husband had the privilege and joy to baptize our eldest grandson. He also had the privilege and joy to baptize our eldest granddaughter. God is good! He continues to bless our grandchildren.

Romans 12:2, directs us to not be conformed to this world but renew our minds with daily scripture reading and then we will know God's will. James 1:2-3 states, "My brethren count it all joy when you fall into various trials, [3] knowing that the testing of your faith produces patience." (NKJV) I have to admit that I did not count the previous trials as all joy when we were going through them. But, we did give praises to God in every situation and shared with others what God had done for us. I have laid bare our lives to enable the reader to see that we, like everyone, experience sin in our lives. We are not perfect, and we all fall short of His Glory at times. There are many people who are reluctant to come to the foot of the cross because they do not feel "good enough." But each of us can have a relationship with our Savior and Lord, Jesus Christ. It doesn't matter to Him our sin. That is the difference. We mess up and God has promised if we seek His forgiveness, He will forgive us. I struggle daily to renew my mind with Godly words and deeds instead of the worldly ones. If truth be told, I'm sure you struggle as most of us do—whether you are Christian or not. So, how do we stop conforming to this world? Step by step with our Savior, Jesus! Sounds simple, doesn't it? The problem for most of us is that we want the abundant life, but we are not willing to be doers. James 1:22, proclaims, "But be doers of the word, and not hearers only, deceiving yourselves." (NKJV) We must put ourselves into action. When we serve the Lord, He will take away the desire to conform to this world. Please allow me to further quote James again as he may have put it best on how to become complete and not tossed about by worldly pleasures.

James 1: 2-6 teaches:

"Count it all joy, my brothers, ²when you meet trials of various kinds, ³for you know that the testing of your faith produces steadfastness. ⁴And let steadfastness have its full effect, that you may be perfect and complete, lacking in nothing. ⁵If any of you lacks wisdom, let him ask God, who gives generously to all without reproach, and it will be given him. ⁶But let him ask in faith, with no doubting, for the one who doubts is like a wave of the sea that is driven and tossed by the wind." (ESV)

Earlier, my oldest daughter was discussing that today's world has created a need to rely on medications with her now seventeen year old son. They were discussing how teens, and adults, have come to think they need medications to deal with their realities, when in reality, they need God! They feel a void in their lives and they fill it with drugs or alcohol or food or anything BUT God and His satiating peace. She related a story from her senior year in college, when she was tempted to take a drug called "No Dose" to stay awake. She explained that she was trying to take classes, hold down a part-time job, and raise her newborn son while living alone and away from her family. It would have been very tempting to take drugs to stay awake and get much needed studying done while her young son slept. However, she recounted to him that she depended on the power of the Holy Spirit to give her the clear mind and fortitude to complete each task daily. She had heard stories of over-the-counter "self-help" drugs unknown and strange effects on people. She had heard of drugs' addictive tendencies. She knew that she didn't need more adversity in her life so she relied on prayer and God's strength to become her saving grace. She communicated to her son that it had not been an easy road, but how the Lord had carried her through it all, without any medications or drugs.

The 2015 generation of teens has a difficult time understanding this concept because they are bombarded with states legalizing marijuana and many mixed messages in society. We now pray daily for our grandchildren to make wise decisions and not be influenced by what seems to be okay in this world. Satan has a way of making those who partake in drugs think they are in control and have the ability to walk away at any time. Satan is a great deceiver. Anyone who has been addicted knows how hard it is to overcome their dependence whether it is drugs, sex or any obsession.

More powerful than our daughter's ability to overcome long hours and studying and raising her son alone, was her faithfulness and trust in God's love and forgiveness. She could have nursed her anger and frustration with hatred, but she held fast to faith, to the positive belief that God had her back, front, sides and all of her so that mother and son could live in fulfillment rather than regret. She has always been tough in spirit but she has ALWAYS believed that nothing was too hard for her because God would never fail her. Her reliance on him has gotten her through raising four children, cervical cancer, spinal surgery, a major real estate investment gone bad, and the normal garden-variety, every-day problems with school, work, neighbors, and etcetera. If all of us could just believe in Him and "let it go" like our eldest daughter can do, our lives could be so much easier. Oh, she would be the first to tell you she struggles daily too!

When we renew our minds and do not conform to this world, but be persistent in our thoughts and actions for Christ, we are stronger, braver, and more capable of fully living. When we strengthen our faith in God, we are unwearied by life's challenges. What darkness do you need to shed? What conformities have you experienced that you should pray over? Write them down. Then, pray.

_____

_____

_____

_____

_____

I have another family story I would share hoping that it may help those of you who have struggled with a divorce. Our youngest daughter's marriage was long unraveling. Her two daughters would keep her committed to making it work. Her labor was constant but her husband's commitment to prayer and therapy or counseling was non-existent. He completely refused to admit there was a problem and he told everyone he definitely was not the cause. Being outside the country, there was too much distance to do anything other than pray for them. We prayed constantly. I prayed that their church would embrace their relationship and that the priest (she married a Catholic and raised her children in the faith of the Catholic Church) would do everything within his power to encourage reconciliation and healing. She was not in her own church of comfort but knew that God exists in most churches or denominations and hoped she could break through the barriers with the priest and his long allegiance to her in-laws. Instead, months of scorn and abandonment seemed to be cast on her by all involved. All of this resulted in her personal insecurities and condemnation from the church leadership. Worse, our grand-daughter's laughter would turn to sadness because they did not witness the love and support they so desperately needed from their father's family for their mother. Our granddaughters felt torn and our youngest daughter could not control what was being said and done in her daughter's presence. Her youngest daughter became very inse-cure and was close to withdrawing from even talking to others. Our daughter sought the advice of a counselor and tried her best to get her husband to go as well. He would not. Actually, he did go one time and announced to the counselor that he didn't have a problem and that "it was his wife's fault." Our daughter was not totally innocent as her frustration gave way to anger and she was quick to yell and argue after years of service to a husband who was betraying her. He became so involved with his own activities he neglected his children and my daughter's emotional needs. He began to emotionally abuse our daughter and eventually this led to an all-out-fight. Since our daughter had police training, she was able to flee without much physical damage, but the emotional and mental anguish was awful. She tried reconciliation—all to no avail. He convinced his parents that it was no fault of his own. What was needed was grace and forgive-ness—but neither came. She was forced to move out of the house to ensure her children did not witness any abuse or the constant arguing that had been evident when she was there. No parent wants to see their children go through such drama. After many hours of us praying, and many tears and her imploring him to go to marriage counseling, her marriage ended in a separation that took three years to finally end in divorce. The separation was almost worse than the marriage as he refused to pay for anything for the children. He refused to grant a divorce because of the beliefs of the Catholic Church. He used the children to try and control our daughter's every wish or need. He would not come to a nearby town where she moved to bring the girls to her. She had to take them to his home which was approximately twenty miles away. She did not ask for child support. Some individuals just want to get what they can, she just wanted out with no strings attached. They worked out a system whereby she would have the girls on her days off as a police officer. While she worked, they would spend time with their daddy. She knew they needed their daddy and maybe this would help him step up and be the dad she knew he could be. She found out later that their girls would be at his parent's house most of the time when he had them. As the girl's matured, this fact was not unnoticed and they began to ask their mother to let them stay longer at her home as "daddy never did anything with them." She would have loved to do so, but because she had become a police officer, she had to work those four days they were away so that she could be home the four days they were with her. It is not what any mother would want but she knew it was a necessity to enable the safety of the girls. It has been nearly five years, but today, the girls are thriving. Our youngest grandchild has again gained her confidence in herself through programs that my daughter enrolled her to help with her insecurities. My daughter is finally regaining her own confidence and finds joy in her new relationship, in her children, in her job and in her friendships that stood by her. She recently married a young man who loves our grandchildren and is excellent with them. It is such a joy to watch him with our grandchildren. They adore him. He has given them the love and support they need to excel in their grades and sports and willingly runs a shuttle service to their school and their biological father. It is my prayer that they all work together for the glory of God.

Some of you may be in a similar battle. Pray daily for guidance. You will need to enlist others to pray for you and your needs as well. Remember to show love and forgiveness in all situations. There are still times the girl's father manipulates by placing a "family" event on a date our daughter has previously cleared. She now hands him a monthly calendar and a weekly calendar with the girls' events on it. She even gives notification of many long-term events as she does not take anything for granted. It is much smoother as she has the events calendar to back up what is going on between their lives.

Our oldest granddaughter was on a traveling basketball team last year and we were privileged to see her play in two games when we were visiting. They actually made it to the championship game for all Ontario and they won! My daughter was honored to have coached them through the championship.

My daughter wanted me to express how she felt when going through her divorce so that others might be aware of some of the pitfalls. She related that she had church going friends and family who were very hypocritical of her actions. They told her she should stay together with her husband and not consider divorce. They were critical of her decision to move out of the house and a few of them abandoned her. What hurts, they were claiming to be Christians. These attitudes gave mixed messages to my daughter and caused her to second guess their faith. She also became disenchanted with organized religion because they placed so much guilt on her. They did not understand all the problems that had incurred within their marriage. A few of the church members, it would seem, could place a false guilt on anyone whom they felt have not measured up to their way of thinking. (Remember Job and what he went through as a believer.) This type of guilt was what my daughter was feeling from those in the church. Jesus showed us this example when the Pharisees brought him a woman caught in adultery. He told them if they were without sin, cast the first stone. In John 8:9-11, we see the perfect example of good guilt. "⁹At this, those who heard began to go away one at a time, the older ones first, until only Jesus was left, with the woman still standing there. ¹⁰Jesus straightened up and asked her, "Woman, where are they? Has no one condemned you?" ¹¹No one, sir," she said. "Then neither do I condemn you," Jesus declared. "Go now and leave your life of sin." Jesus did not condemn. He gave love and hope and a way for redemption. We all need that hope and redemption. It is possible that you felt as my daughter. She is still working through her service to the Lord. She shared that she discusses Jesus with her girls and they talk about God in the beauty of the seasons as they go on hikes very often. I realize that many people today are being "let down" by the organized church. It is because selfishness has crept into the hearts of believers and stolen their joy. We must guard against these kinds of attitudes where we think everyone should "fit" our mold. A woman or man going through a divorce can be looked down on or ridiculed for what they do or say. They need love—not condemnation. You may be feeling judged by others who call themselves Christians. A Christian is not to judge and should love others with an unconditional love. Unfortunately, those who have gone through a divorce may feel the judgment that comes from others.

That condemnation can make them feel "bad" as a person. Instead, we should help those with hurt understand it is their actions that may have been wrong, not themselves. Jesus plainly shared the difference. We tend to be judges. It should not be this way, but because of selfishness it has permeated our society. We can stop these kinds of attitudes with prayer. As Christians, we must seek to get rid of the selfishness in our hearts that condemns others.

When our emotional and spiritual needs as human beings are not being met, when we are unable to inspire love and reconciliation within ourselves, we are in need of the most gracious gift—the immediate and unwavering prayer and support from God's people. David and I continue to pray daily for our children and grandchildren. As I mentioned earlier, we also have others praying for our family. Since God ordered us to love our enemies, how then should we love our friends and family? Sadly, as a culture, we have almost forgotten how to care for others and extend support to our neighbors. Yes, we even pray for our granddaughters' father and his families. We have been instructed in the Bible to pray for those who use us. We are to love the sinner, but hate the sin. Wouldn't this world be better if we all did this? We can be healed ourselves when we pray for others. James 5:16 gives us this great promise, "Confess your trespasses to one another, and pray for one another, that you may be healed. The effective, fervent prayer of a righteous man avails much." (NKJV) This is why I suggest you get others to pray for you and your loved ones. It is vital for your health! Healing can come from those who lift up fervent prayers in righteousness. That is why we still see miracles today.

This is the era of self-promotion. Facebook, Twitter, and snapchat have created a climate of selfishness. We take pictures and post comments of perfection to express our superiority and our grand lives. It becomes extremely hard to see the truth. How are we to see the hurt or pain in someone? How are we to see their need? How are we to help those in need of encouragement? Some people spend countless hours on social media, checking what others are doing and how they might "one-up" their "friends." We seemingly have abandoned civics, community interaction, and our own personal relationships that desperately need repair. We have become a selfish people.

It is evident that people need the Lord when you listen to the nightly news. Rarely do you hear any positive news. Conversely, God's news is supreme—it doesn't matter if there are others by your side. It matters not how many people "follow" you. It matters not how many people make time to offer their love and support. What matters is that God is there for you and YOU follow HIM. He has a plan for you as found in Jeremiah 29,

[11]"For I know the plans I have for you," declares the Lord, "plans to prosper you and not to harm you, plans to give you hope and a future. [12]Then you will call on me and come and pray to me, and I will listen to you. [13]You will seek me and find me when you seek me with all your heart. [14]I will be found by you, "declares the Lord," (Jeremiah 29: 11-14 NIV)

In a world where everyone has the notion that if it doesn't work out, we'll just quit, how do we nurture relationships that are lasting, relationships on which we can depend on the other person to carry that yoke with us? When the relationships that are promoted are the twenty second blurbs on social media, how do we foster relationships that last a lifetime? How will we maintain love and respect when praying regularly with the one we love is an afterthought or not at all. The only way we can foster lasting relationships is to learn to pray as Jesus has exemplified in His time here on earth. God has promised He will listen to us. Jeremiah was told by God that if he sought Him with all his heart, he would be found. We too can claim this promise! We must learn to pray together and make the time to pray together. When was the last time you and your loved one prayed together? I do not mean at mealtime. When did you get together and lift up your children or someone in your family? There is an old saying, "Those who pray together, stay together!" And, it is TRUE! David and I have been married for forty-four years. It keeps getting better! I would love to tell you that it has been a constant journey of bliss and understanding. There definitely have been more ups than downs. There has been a love that has persevered because we both sought the Lord. Through all the trials, I never lost faith that God was in control of my life. There is a country song that tells us that it takes a little rain to make love grow. It does take those trials and hurtful times to help us appreciate the good times in life and marriage. We grow when we listen to the needs of our loved ones. We grow when we listen to the Lord.

Are you listening to the Spirit of the Lord? What is He telling you? The soul is made up of the mind, emotion and the will. You see, God wants all of our being, not just a portion of our devotion. It is that way with our loved ones too. They want and need our devotion. They need our prayers daily! And, they need us to pray with them! In today's world, self-empowerment and self-fulfillment have resulted in relationships where we tend to selfishly feel the marriage should revolve around us. It's hard to juggle all our daily tasks and still make room to think about the needs of one another. So, here's a challenge: you and your spouse make at least five minutes for heartfelt discussion. This can be morning or evening. You come to the discussion with one need/idea; your spouse comes with their own need/idea. You lift those desires up in prayer and you determine how you can go about achieving them together with God. Let's call this a "Mini Huddle." Forgive my football reference—but what do you expect from the footballer's wife? We'll discuss this more in a later chapter so I would like to discuss in my next chapter how to identify your God given gifts. Some of you may not know your gift! However, before you think about your gifts, make a list of all the people in your life you should lift up in prayers daily. Take one moment to right down any needs these people have so you can be specific in lifting them up:

_____

_____

_____

_____

_____

_____

_____

You may be struggling with raising your own children or grand-children. I only raised three daughters. The teen years made me weary. There are many couples that never get out of the teen years together. Only through much prayer being lifted by us together, and by our prayer warriors, could we make it out as a couple. Go back to the beginning of this chapter and claim the promise that God made. He will give you rest if we just come to Him. It could be you have other needs that are not being met. Philippians 4:19 is a promise to you: "And my God shall supply all your need according to His riches in glory by Christ Jesus." (NKJV) Write down your needs. Write down how you are wearied. Think about how God is directing you to meet those needs. Then, write the name(s) of one or two people who can pray for those needs. Seek out those people and ask for their prayer support. Pray with them.

_____

_____

_____

_____

_____

_____

# Chapter Nine

# Identify Your God Given Gifts

"⁶We have different gifts, according to the grace given us. If a man's gift is prophesying, let him use it in proportion to his faith. ⁷If it is serving, let him serve; if it is teaching let him teach; ⁸if it is encouraging, let him encourage; if it is contributing to the needs of others, let him give generously; if it is leadership, let him govern diligently; if it is showing mercy, let him do it cheerfully." (Romans 12:6-8 NIV)

There was no color on the cold drab concrete brick walls. The lighting was dim as if to hide the dreariness and utter hopelessness of those moving slowly down a decrepit corridor to a large brighter room where someone would proclaim the Word of God. Clank! What an awful sound as the man of God was let into the solitude of the prison. Have you ever visited someone inside a prison or jail? I have not. Oh, I did take a group of middle school students on a field trip to a local county jail once. I definitely did not want to go back. But, my husband was involved in a jail ministry for several years with a Christian friend of his. My husband shared with me about that experience. He considered it a very special ministry. His friend said it was his calling and that God had given him the gift of encouraging those who found themselves behind bars.

I have not been called to visit those in prison—yet. I love to cheer people into successful roles of service in the church. I also love to help others find their God given gifts. I find myself looking for ways to enable others to be whatever it is they want to be. I also love to be the one who stays after a church-wide meal and wipe down the tables and put up the chairs. I love to be a helper. There have been occasions where I have had to take the lead and plan an event. I can do this, but I tend to wait to the last minute to complete my tasks and that stresses out my husband. Realizing this, I usually look for someone to place into a position to accomplish the task with my help rather than taking the credit. I am satisfied to be on a team and I do not have to be the one in charge. That in itself is a gift. There are so many chiefs in this world that need to be in control and need the recognition of being the one in control. It is my nature to be a peacemaker and I enjoy leading through example and encouraging someone else to take control.

You probably already have an idea of what some of your gifts are. You may have chosen your profession based on the knowledge of what you enjoyed and did well. I became a teacher. A teacher is a public servant who must educate and mediate on a daily basis. While in public education, I witnessed the love of Jesus through my actions of loving my students unconditionally. Every single year, there would be students who would raise their hands and say something like, "You are a Christian, aren't you, Mrs. Walters?" For the thirty years I taught, there would be students who wanted to come live with my family as they felt that love. It was humbling, yet heartbreaking. I could not share with them about salvation unless specifically asked. As the years progressed, all rights of personal expression were taken away as I could not give hope as "it might infringe on someone else's right." There were many times I gave hope to those who needed it by choosing my words carefully. The last several years, before I retired, I was called into the Principals' office in regard to some moral or ethical truth I had delivered to my students. On one such occasion, I was scolded because I heard a student say inappropriate language at another student and when I interjected that these words were demeaning and not appropriate for school, the student defended his blasphemous words by claiming his parents spoke like that to him 'all the time!' Without thinking I replied, "Your parents shouldn't direct that type of language at you and you shouldn't direct it at others." The parents actually came to school upset because I tried to teach their child morals that did not agree with their own. I asked them if they would like for me to say those same words to them and of course they replied with more curse words that they would not. No wonder our society is decaying and we see constant school shootings and murder rates have risen in our cities. It is called selfishness.

The last few years I taught, I was determined to make as much a difference as I could. Each day was such a joy as I not only taught my curriculum, but I taught a "safe" environment concept. No one was allowed to be put down in class and if someone had a bad thing happen in the class before, we stopped to discuss how it made us feel and what we could do to get us back on track to learn again. Many students wanted to come to my class because they knew I did not yell or raise my voice at them when they misbehaved. I had them tell me what they needed to do to obey those rules that had been broken. We discussed how it affected each person in the room. It wasn't long before the assistant principal would call me to see if I could take a student who would not comply in another classroom into my own classroom. When the students found out I was retiring, they begged me to stay. But I knew it was time for me to step down and let a younger generation fight the battles of public education. The world no longer offers freedom of speech in education as you have to be too politically correct. I would retire to pen my witness to the world. Oh, I dearly miss those eager faces that wanted to be loved and hugged. God has given me new faces to hug and love in my new church family. It is a joy to help others see their potential to serve the Lord.

To serve Christ, you must come to know the will of God for your life. Many people go through life with a void because they do not realize that they **need** to understand the will of God. So many are tripped up because they search for meaning in worldly pleasures that make them "feel" good. We may all proclaim, "Been there, done that!" If you do not know where you are going, how can you find God's will for your life? I heard in a recent movie that if you wanted to hit a target at 300 yards, you had to use a rifle and not a scatter gun. By the same design, you must target your faith to find the will of the

Lord so you will know how to direct your life. Do you know God's will for your life? How do you find God's will?

First, **pray that God will show you His will for your life**. Jesus tells us how to find His will in John 7:17, "If anyone wills to do His will, he shall know concerning the doctrine, whether it is from God or whether I speak on My own authority."(NKJV) We must be in God's Word. Then, you must claim the promise in Mark 11:24 where Jesus promises, "Therefore I say to you, whatever things you ask when you pray, believe that you receive them, and you will have them." (NKJV) Once you have made this request, reflect upon what you do well and the things you aren't as capable. Make a list of your strengths and then ask others for their ideas and see if they match up. If you think you are gifted as a Sunday school teacher and no one else thinks you are gifted in that area, guess what? You need to reconsider. Someone might tell you that you have a nice voice and you need to join the choir. You should join the choir! If you think you have the gift of leadership, look behind you to see who is following. If no one is there, you are not a leader. You will never know what you are good at until you try!

Second, **try different ministry areas.** You need to ask yourself a couple of questions before you jump into serving. You might ask yourself, "Where have I served and people confirmed I did a good job?" If you joined the choir and others are glad you are there to serve, then the chances are good it is God's will you sing in the choir. If you love working in the nursery, then sign up to work in the nursery to see if that truly is your calling. If you chair a committee and lead it to success and are given compliments for your efforts, then you know you have the gift of leadership. The more mature you become in Christ, the more gifts He gives you. You may find yourself giving generously out of the little you have because God knows you have a generous heart. You must experiment in different areas of service in order to know those areas that bring you the most joy in living. By the same token, I'm sure you have known of committees that are dominated by someone who wants to have things their way and thrive on that control. It is not God's will that we control anything! In Ephesians 5:17 Paul relates, "Therefore do not be unwise, but understand what the will of the Lord is." (NKJV) In other words, try to find out and do whatever the Lord wants you to do. You are to be wise and understand what the will of God is for you. We must learn to be excellent stewards of God's time and talents. We must be wise about our service to the Lord.

Third, **start serving**! You will never know what you are gifted with until you sign up for service. Don't try to figure out your gifts until you volunteer to serve in an area you really think you will love. You will learn what is best for you. You must consider your heart and personality. Are you a team player or do you like to work alone? Are you a behind the scenes person, or do you like to hear immediate praise and feedback? These are just a few questions you should ask yourself when considering service. It is time for you to write down what God has revealed to you as a service area. Write down all the ways you think you may be of service to the Lord. If you are still not sure, ask a trusted believer to pray with you and help you find that area of service. Then, prayerfully consider how you can serve and just do it!

_____

_____

_____

_____

_____

_____

It is at this point I may need to give you a warning. You can get so wrapped up in your service that you become selfish. God knew this! He had Paul urge the Ephesians to walk in unity as the body of Christ. Paul went on to teach that Christ gave each of us special abilities from His rich storehouse of gifts. (Ephesians: 4) Paul is imploring all Christians to get rid of deceitful desires, watch our attitudes, get rid of bitterness, not let the sun go down on our anger, and forgive each other just as Christ forgave us. It is these later verses in Chapter four and the beginning of Chapter five we need to read daily. We are encouraged to repent of our selfishness. Take the challenge! Read these two chapters daily for the next week, and pray for a loving heart. The Word of God will change your life. These chapters might prove too much for you to digest all at once. Try only portions of the two chapters. Live out those truths for Jesus. Allow yourself to engage more of the Truths in your daily living. How you treat significant others and family members and church family is embellished in these two chapters. Again, take this challenge and you will find and live true joy! You will find God's will for your life. Write down how you can unify your walk with Jesus and your families (biological, church, work related, and any other significant others in your life.) Also, write a prayer to God asking for forgiveness where conviction came while reading the two chapters in Ephesians. Your relationship to the people you love will become stronger. Your relationship to those you considered your enemies will be changed and you will be able to love those you deemed unlovable. Remember, all things are possible through Jesus!

_____

_____

_____

_____

_____

_____

Prayers: _____

_____

_____

_____

_____

# Chapter Ten

# Value Yourself!
## (Take Your Own Selfie)

"Examine me, O Lord, and prove me; Try my mind and my heart." (Psalm 26:2 NKJV)

"But let a man examine himself, and so let him eat of the bread and drink of the cup." (1 Corinthians 11:28 NKJV)

L ife is unpredictable! Just when we have a very important engage-ment we want to attend, a record setting snow storm sets in and cancels your plans. No matter what the circumstances are that change your plans, disappointment sets in. How do we handle the obstacles life throws at us? Do we even consider offering up a similar prayer as David did to the Lord in Psalm 26:2-3? Do we ask God to examine us? Do we even stop to examine ourselves? Most of us would have to say no. It is our selfish nature to try and handle all our problems on our own. Unfortunately, unless we are renewing our minds daily with the Word of

God, we don't give prayer a fleeting thought. Why is that? Do you have a relationship with God on a daily basis? Be truthful and answer each of these questions honestly. We all have selfish desires we need to examine.

Whether you want to admit it or not, God tells us in Proverbs that if we spare the rod, we spoil the child. God did not tell us to put the young child in time out. (I am not saying there is not a time or place for doing so. It is how you teach after the time out has been observed that matters.) Some of you may already be screaming, "But what about the abuse?" God did not intend for us to abuse our children either. We are to train up our children. This is scriptural. The problem is we do not train! Allow me to share a typical scenario.

The three year old son was pitching a huge tantrum. He declared to his mother that he was not going to Sunday school. She pleaded with him to settle down. She argued that he would love his class once he got there. Her son proceeded to take off all his church clothes down to his underwear. She countered by saying she knew he would love to hear the stories of Jesus. He blurted out, "No way! I hate my teacher!" The mother shouted and gruffly grabbed her son by the arm, "Young man, you are in time out!" Sound familiar? This could have happened in your home. Whether this or a similar event has or hasn't happened in your life, let us first examine the verbiage with our children.

Are you in the habit of explaining why your child was in time-out? Do you take the time to train? Do you talk to your children about Godly principals? Those of you who do so, may God bless your efforts! You have been taught the value of sharing with your child spiritual truths. Examine yourself. Feeling guilty? I know I had to do some repentance here. Most of us are guilty of being in such a hurry to accomplish the next task, we neglect to train effectively. If you are constantly telling your young child to not do this and "no" on that without discussing the Biblical truths that might apply to the situation, then you are losing the worldly battle. We must learn to redirect our young children with Godly principles and examples. How did Jesus teach? With examples! This is the will of God that we learn this truth.

When my girls were young, I did not spare the switch. Mostly, they remember my Godly mother, their grandmother, using that switch. But, she didn't just stop at the switch. She taught lessons about the consequences of their actions. I tried to mimic her discipline. I had good intentions about teaching with lessons every time. Like I have stated previously, I have to admit that I failed to be consistent. I thought my inability to concentrate for periods of time and having a mind that got off task easily wreaked havoc with teaching life lessons. Or, was that just an excuse? Yes, I had problems focusing. However, that too could be put into remission by the renewing of my mind with God's Word. I really had no excuse! Nevertheless, it would take me many years before I would realize this and give it to God. If you ask my husband, I still need help in being consistent. Please, don't let this happen to you. My children were fortunate to have a father who taught with examples. You may have children who are already six or older and they may defy you at every turn. It is never too late! Prayer and the help of God can help you to teach your children with examples. You can do God's will.

Consequently, you must examine yourself and be willing to change your life. Did you get that? You must be willing to change your life.

Accordingly, you might be asking, "How can I do this?" Are you letting Ephesians chapter four and five change you? You can learn to take your everyday ordinary life and place it before the Lord as an offering. To do this, you need to take a look at your values. How do you react when your world is spiraling out of control? I hope you react with prayer and a positive hope and action enables you to succeed. On the other hand, you may be one who yells, curses, or reacts in such a negative way others avoid or tend to get out of your way. Are you smiling? Did you like the fact that others run from your wrath? You may need to take a glimpse into the values that God would have you possess. I am going to allow you to take this journey thru an acrostic using the letters from the word—values.

The letter "V" stands for vessel. You are a vessel. You fill your vessel daily with many thoughts, feelings, and chatter from this world. With what are you filling your vessel? In a letter to the Thessalonians, Paul implores in 1 Thessalonians 4:4, ". . .that each of you should know how to possess his own vessel in sanctification and honor." We must have a body that is filled with honor. We cannot allow passions and lust of the world to dwell in our vessel. Paul, in verse five, states that this would be like those who do not know God. Anything that takes us away from the passion of serving Christ is a worldly passion. It would be like the lady I once knew in my Bible study class. She came to exercise and Bible study one day a week in my gym. But while there, she would talk about going to Bingo three nights a week and even having a babysitter come over on one night because her husband couldn't keep the kids that night. Bingo was so much fun and she actually would win at least once a week. As she studied the Word of God, she realized she had an addiction to Bingo and that she didn't need the smoke-filled room because of her health. I would love to tell you she quit Bingo and that she chose to fill her vessel with Godly thoughts. It is just not true. She agonized over giving up Bingo one day after Bible study and I thought she was going to give it up after prayer. Instead, we did not see her again at Bible study. At that time in her life, she valued that worldly pleasure more than studying God's Word. Again, look at yourself and see how you are filling your vessel. In Acts 9:15, Jesus assures Ananias that Paul is His chosen vessel. We can pray for the Lord to use us as His vessel to proclaim the gospel to our family and friends and even to the whole world. Just like Paul, we will have to continually ask forgiveness and clean our vessel. We would not think of eating meals off the same plate without cleaning our plate after each meal. It would make us sick. It could even kill us! Neither should we let our earthly vessel (ourselves) become unclean. That is one reason why there is so much sickness among us. We neglect to clean our vessel daily and purify our service to Jesus. Again, I am going to give you a few lines to purify your vessel. Ask God to take away any worldly pleasures that come from your selfish nature.

_____

_____

_____

_____

_____

The second letter in values is the "A." After you have cleansed your vessel, you can deal with others **affectionately.** In Romans 12:10 we are given directions of how to conduct ourselves as a Christian, "Be kindly affectionate to one another with brotherly love, in honor giving preference to one another;" We are to love our neighbor as ourselves! As Christians, we should know this. Yet, giving affection for others is harder when dealing with real life situations. I'm reminded of this Truth while watching the news. I was horrified as I watched ISIS behead Christians in the name of Allah. I was saddened as I watched people from Ferguson, Missouri mention in an interview that they felt nothing when two policemen were shot. When I listen to the news, it would seem all I hear anymore is the killing of innocent people because someone feels they have been done wrong. Our world is not practicing brotherly love. Are you practicing brotherly love on a daily basis? Are you giving preference to those who you consider your friends? What about those who are not your friends? What about the people where you have differing opinions? We must learn to love others affectionately even when we do not agree with their ideas. We all have the selfish desire to be treated as an equal. However, we need to realize that all mankind will never be equal except at the foot of the cross. Jesus told us the poor would always be with us. We are to minister to their needs. There is nothing wrong with our desire to be treated fairly. But, we must be willing to treat the person who is treating us without respect with brotherly love and respect. Oh, did I step on your toes? Remember earlier I shared how Jesus taught us through examples. He said to turn the other cheek. Scriptures tell us to go the extra mile and love others who do not love you. Instead of the streets being filled with protestors, our churches need to be filled with those who need to learn what real love is. Our churches need to be filled with those who realize they have a tangible need to get rid of selfish desires and replace them with affectionate ones. The church in Charleston, South Carolina exemplified the forgiveness of Christ to the world when they openly forgave the young man who killed their loved ones. There have been some Godly individuals interviewed about what is happening to heal lives in Ferguson, Charleston, and the Middle East, but the media very rarely covers those stories. Human selfishness seems to govern the chaos. You only hear the negative and hatred portrayed by individuals. I do admire those individuals on Facebook, twitter, or other social media's that give a Christian testimony in what they post or say. They promote affectionate brotherly love. It is encouraging to have friends who post more positive than negative. What about you? Do your friends post positive thoughts? Or, do you find that most of what you read on Facebook is negative? If it is, you need to find more friends who are positive. Those who treat you affectionately are genuine friends. When you treat others with affection, then you are a true and authentic friend. Do you need to become more affectionate? Write on the lines below how you can do this and then pray you treat others with brotherly love.

_____

_____

_____

_____

_____

The third letter in values is "L." The L stands for **longsuffering**. You might ask, what is longsuffering? It is forgiving someone and being tolerant of their methods or dialogue. When you are practicing longsuffering, you are completely selfless. In Ephesians 4:2, Paul implores the Ephesians to walk in unity with their fellow Christian friends, ". . .with all lowliness and gentleness, with longsuffering, bearing with one another in love. . ." As you practice longsuffering, you are practicing a tolerant love for others who may not return the same tolerance to you. Does it grate on your nerves when the person you are talking to breaks in on almost every sentence you verbalize? They may say something like, "Exactly, I. . ." and go on to expound upon their knowledge to the point that you deem them a "know it all." You may even become frustrated when they have interrupted three or more times. However, this is the person who I am referring to who needs your longsuffering attitude of love. I'm sure you have been confiding in a friend and another acquaintance walks up to you both and demands to know what you were talking about. They exhibit no common courtesy. Again, this is where you need to prac-tice longsuffering. You do not need to share what it is that you were confiding with your friend. However, you can lovingly share another story with this person so that they feel included. Unfortunately, there are those who tell others it is none of their business and alienate others as if they are unimportant. They are not accommodating the needs of another human being. To be selfless and not selfish, you must practice longsuffering. It brings to mind all the bullying I have witnessed in teaching middle school. Bullying tears at the very core of an individual's need to be accepted and loved. As parents, you need to teach your children longsuffering. You need to discuss with them that everyone, no matter their race, ethnic background, or sexual orientation, needs to be accepted and loved as Jesus accepts and loves us all unconditionally. You may not agree with their beliefs, but in order to show true love and selflessness, you must learn to accept them as they are. When you do this, God will convict them where they need conviction. God made it clear that we are not to judge—only love. Christians are to hate the sin, but love the sinner! I have given you a time to write down your thoughts. Are you judgmental toward someone? Write down how you can become more accepting and forgiving—practicing longsuffering. Pray over what you have written.

_____

_____

_____

_____

_____

_____

The fourth letter in values is the "U." I've already alluded to the fact that we need to walk as one. We need to love others in the **unity of Christ.** Paul announces in Ephesians 4:3 that we need to endeavor to keep the unity of the Spirit in the bond of peace. Paul knew if a church is to grow, then all its' members must be unified and serving in peace. What happens when a member decides that they do not like what the others have voted to do? We see that person talking to others and getting them to side with their point of view. Soon we have two factions that cannot agree and unless they pray and ask forgiveness, we have a split. God knew we were selfish. That is why in Ephesians 4:14 Paul exclaims, ". . .that we should no longer be children, tossed to and fro and carried about with every wind of doctrine, by the trickery of men, in the cunning craftiness of deceitful plotting, 15but, speaking the truth in love,. . ." (NKJV) We are to be unified in Christ and His love. How then can people be tricked into following someone like a Jim Jones or more recently an organization like ISIS? It is mind boggling to me how anyone, particularly a woman, would want to follow a group of radicals that behead people! They do not allow women to hold a position of authority nor do they allow women to even show their face in public. Jesus came to free us of the deceitful plotting of men. It is sad many are blinded by their selfish nature of trickery and deceitful plotting against those who proclaim unity in love. Please pray for these people to come to the cross of Jesus and receive the salvation that can be theirs. We need to claim the promise in 2 Chronicles 7:14, "if My people who are called by My name will humble themselves, and pray and seek My face, and turn from their wicked ways, then I will hear from heaven and will forgive their sin and heal their land." America was founded upon unifying principles and values. We as individual's, can become unified in the love of God. We need to claim this promise and return to Godly principles. This Old Testament promise can still be claimed by Christians today. I challenge you to write down your thoughts where you can unify Godly principles and then pray this prayer for our land to be healed. Also, you may need to confess where you have been a divider in your church life.

_____

_____

_____

_____

_____

_____

The fifth letter of values is the "E." We need to pray in **earnest.** James 5:17 gives an Old Testament example where it says, "Elijah was a man with a nature like ours, and he prayed earnestly that it would not rain; and it did not rain on the land for three years and six months." (NKJV) Notice that James said Elijah had a nature like ours. He was not perfect! He was a man who had failings and selfish desires just like us. Where he was different was that he prayed in earnest. He was so serious about his prayer that he sincerely knew that God would answer his prayer. It was heartfelt! Do you offer up heartfelt prayers? Do you come before the throne of God with such expectation that your prayers are intense and asking for God's will to be done? We can have that power! Please allow me to digress to a time in our lives when David and I experienced this power. I was pregnant with my second daughter and David had just taken a coaching job in Bardstown, Kentucky. We had a home that we were trying to sell in the late seventies. It was not the best of times to sell, but I began praying for someone to buy our house in Glasgow. In order to have any capital to put a payment down on another house, we needed a home in the price range of $25,000. We had looked and looked and could not find such a house unless we bought a newly constructed house several miles away from the city. Even then, it was in the low forty's. Having one little girl about to turn two and another on the way made that home seem too far away from where David would be spending all his time—Bardstown high school. Because we did not seem to have any other options, David put down some good faith money on the home under construction. What woman would not want the possibility of finalizing the construction of her new home? I did not. I did not like the idea of being so far out of town and knowing how football would not allow my husband to come home until very late. My children and I would be trapped in the country with no stores to walk to nor any neighbors as no one had moved into the area yet. For those of you who do not understand—there were no cell phones! I began to earnestly pray for a home to come available in town close to the school. One night, I was asleep when I became aware that I was very hot and saw a bright light enter the room. I felt a presence that I cannot explain other than I believe it was an angel of the Lord. He showed me a picture of a small yellow Cape Cod house with a bicycle out front and a man walking into the front yard with a "for sale" sign in his hand. The man said his house would be selling for $25,000. Although I was very hot, I had goose bumps all over my body when I woke up! I could not sleep after that vision. I called my sister-in-law to babysit my two year old and got on the road from Glasgow to Bardstown. When you drive into Bardstown from Hodgenville, you turn right in front of the Catholic

Church and the first light leads to the high school where David would be teaching and coaching. For some reason, I went to the second light and turned left onto 4th street. I really did not know the city very well and was slowly proceeding down the street looking for the house in my vision. I had covered a couple of blocks when all of a sudden, on my left, I saw a small yellow Cape Cod house with a bicycle out front. I got those goose bumps again! I stopped the car in the middle of the street and jumped out of my car as a man came around from the back with a "For Sale" sign in his hands! You guessed it! I ran up to him and blurted out how much was he selling the house for? He said something about the owner dying from cancer and the children wanted a quick sale so they had decided to place only $25,000 on it to get rid of it as soon as possible. I told him it was sold! Don't bother to stick the sign in the yard as I was going to drive over one block to the high school and retrieve my husband and we would be buying this house! I had not even seen the inside! I did not need to. I knew the Lord had provided!

I had called David that morning to tell him that I had the vision and explained to him that I was coming to find the house. Needless to say, my husband was in awe of how God had delivered our next home into our possession. On top of that, the homes around us had been sold with a much higher value. Not only did God deliver us a home in town at the right price, but within the next weeks, He also had us a buyer for our home in Glasgow. Lifting up prayer earnestly with an unfailing expectation of it being answered in God's will gets results! Scriptures promise us God will answer those earnest prayers. He has been faithful to answer each one of those prayers for us. I just have to share one more of these!

You see, the daughter that I was carrying, our middle child, would have a special need for healing at age twenty-three. She had finished college and had just returned from an archeological dig in Italy. She had aged out for being on our insurance policy at the time. She was having abdominal pain. We didn't have much extra money for doctor bills but told her to go to my gynecologist for evaluation. He discovered a huge tumor on one of her ovaries. It measured eight and a half centimeters. The doctor wanted to operate immediately as he needed to take a biopsy to determine if it was cancerous. David and I set up the appointment for surgery with my gynecologist. He told us if we believed in the power of prayer we should pray for a miracle. We prayed earnestly that God would heal her miraculously and she would not need the surgery. We also had hundreds of others praying for a miracle. The day of the surgery came and my doctor sent his intern to talk with us since he was in another surgery. I was hoping they would check our daughter before she went into surgery. Hospitals get so busy and you know how interns are sometimes allowed to get a patient ready and the surgeon shows up at the last minute to actually complete the surgery. They opened her abdomen to find, you guessed it, nothing! My doctor was floored and apologetic! I was not mad and again told him that we had prayed for this miracle. He shared with us that in his thirty years of practice it was the first time to his knowledge someone had prayed for a miracle and received it. I praised the Lord right there in the lobby! He could not get over how an eight and a half centimeter tumor had disappeared! But we all knew. God had answered our earnest prayer for healing once again. Not only that, but my doctor totally wrote off his bill and the hospital did not send charges as well! The only bill we had to pay was the anesthesiologist bill.

Do you believe you can pray an earnest prayer and God will answer according to His will? I do! It is time to search your heart and write down what you earnestly need God to do in your life. The key is praying in His will and believing! Luke 11: 9 tells us to ask and it will be given to us. Do you truly believe? Again, Matthew 21:22, tells us that whatever we ask, believing, we will receive. God tells you that if you have the faith of a mustard seed that you can move mountains. Do you truly believe? You must ask in earnest to receive. Ask here:

_____

_____

_____

_____

_____

_____

Now I come to the last letter of the acrostic—values. The "S" stands for **strengthen**. We are to strengthen each other. Because God knew we would have days we were depressed or not feeling as confident as we should, He implored us to strengthen each other. We find this command in several places in both the Old and New Testaments. In Luke 22:32, Jesus lets us know He is praying for us! He says to Peter, "But I have prayed for you, that your faith should not fail; and when you have returned to Me, strengthen your brethren." (NKJV) Jesus knew beforehand that Peter was going to deny Him three times. But Jesus still prayed when Peter realized what he had done and he returned to Jesus, that he would also strengthen the others by sharing his shortcomings. You and I can share how we are not perfect—only Jesus. In a world that tears down and depreciates individuals by bullying, making fun of, and even murder, we need to be strengthened. If you have so called "friends" that make you feel inferior or sad in any way, you need to search out those individuals who will lift you up and flee from those who would tear you down. Don't allow yourself to be in a relationship where you feel uncomfortable and belittled. If you are in a relationship where you are being abused physically or emotionally, you need to seek a Christian friend who will strengthen you through prayers and friendship. You should never have to endure such treatment. I'm reminded of a case that I heard about many years ago where a woman was being emotionally abused. The children were being physically abused. The abuse was borderline and hard to prove. It was hard to make a case against the abuser. Then one night, the abuser snapped and held a gun to one of her children's head and threatened to pull the trigger. The frightened woman gathered her children that night and left the home. She never went back to that situation again. She previously had tried to work out her marriage with counseling and the strength of others from her church. Her husband would not change. Oh, he pleaded and said he would change and that he would get help to never commit those things again. But, the night when he pulled the gun, finally woke her up to the realization she needed to be strengthened, not demeaned and continually put down or frightened for her life or those of her children. She went back to college to receive a degree and a profession of her own. She found friends who would strengthen her, not put her down.

You need friends who strengthen you. Remember that "mini huddle" I discussed earlier? I do hope you have a significant other or husband with whom you can pray. So that peace will be a part of your life, you need to have five to fifteen minutes daily with the one you love. You need to make the time to share your feelings, needs and wants with the one you love. Your life will take on a new meaning when you can do this. You will gain a strength you never thought possible. It is my prayer that you can name all the people who strengthen you. Say a prayer of thanksgiving for such good friends. If you cannot think of people who strengthen you, please find a local church and flee from that bondage of hurt and pain. Go back and re-read chapter eight and be transformed daily by the renewing of your mind in God's Word. Serve Jesus in a church so that you can identify your God given gifts. Yes, examine yourself by using the values acrostic. Make a plan of action if you do not have one! Please take a "selfie!" Begin writing your plan of action here:

_____

_____

_____

_____

_____

_____

# Chapter Eleven

# Pray Without Ceasing!

". . .Pray without ceasing,. . ." (1 Thessalonians 5:17 NKJV)

J ust do it! We have used this phrase so many times in so many situations. It is true—we must overcome selfishness by praying without ceasing. Just do it! Jesus intended for us to talk to Him about everything. First, it is evident God intended for us to pray in our rising up and our laying down. David, the Psalmist, wrote in Psalm 55:17, "Evening and morning and at noon I will pray, and cry aloud, And He shall hear my voice." (NKJV) Many of us teach our children to pray at mealtimes. This would follow with the teaching the Psalmist, David, set forth. However, I'm afraid our prayers at mealtime have become more rote and without conviction. Yes, we need to teach young children easy prayers to recite at the table, but they should not be the only prayers offered. We need to allow our children to hear adult voices praising God for the blessings we have and asking God for help in times of trouble. These prayers help us to keep our selfish ways in check. So, let's see. . .do you pray at least three times daily? Ouch! There are some days I must admit that I have not gone before the throne of God until bedtime. Then, there are others where I started the day with my Savior, Jesus, and then got so busy with worldly events and never returned to thank Him or even end the day with Him. I tumbled into bed exhausted for sleep and did not even think of talking to Jesus or praising Him for the blessings of the day. How could I be so selfish? After all, He is my creator and Savior! He is your creator. He is our friend and comforter. Why do we not treat Him as such? We wouldn't think of going a day without getting on Facebook and sharing things with our earthly friends. The answer is rather simple—selfishness!

Like I stated before, we get so wrapped up in thinking about all the worldly things we need to do at work today, or how we need to clean out our closets or who we need to contact to repair the plumbing. We worry about getting a babysitter because we have a meeting after school or must pull an extra shift at work unannounced. We can't decide what to wear to the movies to meet our friends or what restaurant to eat at because we want one thing while our partner or friend wants another. Now all of these things are important to us. But, do we ever have a conversation with Jesus to ask His opinion or get His help on what we should do? When we do, we can overcome selfishness. There are many scriptures that teach us how to effectively use prayer in our lives to enable us to have the joy of the Lord daily. Let's take a look at several of these.

The second evidence we have for how to pray is found from Romans. "For we do not know what we should pray for as we ought, but the Spirit Himself makes intercession for us with groanings which cannot be uttered." (Romans 8:26b NKJV) I don't know about you, but I have problems knowing what to pray for at different times. God knew we would not know how to pray! Isn't it wonderful? God has given us another gift—the Holy Spirit who helps in our weaknesses. Romans 8: 26, is truly comforting! Especially when I go to sleep exhausted! The Holy Spirt groans for me. It is one of those verses we should commit to memory. God's grace and love is complete. He has thought of all the imperfections we struggle with daily and has given us scriptures to help us become more Christ-like and to have joy in the Lord. Our problem is that we let our "playbook" collect dust! When was the last time you opened your Bible? Do you know where it is? Can you imagine what would happen if an NFL player did not memorize his playbook and know all his assignments? He would lose all the money invested in him and have to pack his bags and leave.

The third evidence for prayer is to overcome temptation. We self-ishly take our Savior for granted. The ultimate price has been paid for us and we let dust collect on our Bibles! We neglect to talk to our redeemer and friend! Yes, Jesus is our friend who we can talk to and confide all our problems and successes. Subsequently, we must pray without ceasing to overcome our selfishness. In Matthew 26: 41, Jesus understood our humanness when He implored His disciples to, "Watch and pray, lest you enter into temptation. The spirit indeed is willing, but the flesh is weak." (NKJV) I don't know about you, but I must continually watch my fleshly desires. I must pray about my relationship with my husband and children and grandchildren. If I don't do this, I find myself interjecting thoughts and talk that is not Godly in nature. We must also watch our talk at church. I remember a time at church when I was discussing a Biblical truth with another church member and I became adamant about what I thought to be the Truth. At the time, I was selfishly proving my point according to scriptures from my perspective. She was looking at the issue from her perspective. Who was correct? Neither of us! After I had left the situation, I had to repent of my selfishness. I went to her later and asked her to forgive my condescending tone. Each of us must study the Word of God and scriptures are revealed as we study. What we believe has been revealed to us can actually take on a different interpretation as we again study God's Word. That is growing in His Word. We must remember, some mysteries will be revealed in Heaven.

Accordingly, one of our biggest struggles comes from the physical realm. The forth evidence that God shares about our need for prayer is our fleshly nature. We desire to eat too much. We love pizza buffets because we can really get our monies worth and it tastes so good. My weakness is the desert after the meal. My father had to end every meal with something sweet. I grew up thinking I needed to fill that "sweet tooth" as well. We also lust after the things that make us feel good. For some people it is a cigarette. For others it is an alcoholic beverage or any substance that gives a euphoric feeling that tends to make us "not feel" inferior or sad or stressed. We justify that we just want to relax. Another example would be those who have a sexual lust and become slaves to their fantasies or sexual desires. They may seek magazines or books or movies and media to fulfill these desires. I believe in recent years one of the biggest downfalls in our physical struggles has come with our talk. Do you curse? Do you use the Lord's name in vain? God knew we would have problems with our tongue. God's Word addresses this in James 5:12, "But above all, my brethren, do not swear, either by heaven or by earth or with any other oath. But let your "Yes" be "Yes," and your "No," "No," lest you fall into judgment." (NKJV) This command is harsh. You may want to examine your talk. Take a selfie! Are your words condemning you into judgment? You do not have to feel guilty. Ask for forgiveness right now! Jesus, in His infinite wisdom, knew that we would need to pray about our weaknesses. Even as He was going to the cross, He prayed without ceasing. He asked His disciples to do the same. They could not! They tried. But, they went to sleep when Jesus needed them the most. We too must attempt to pray without ceasing so that Jesus can erase our physical, mental and emotional weaknesses each and every day. Have you identified your strengths and "weaknesses?" As you identify them, are you asking the Lord to show you how to confess and change those weaknesses? Here are a couple of lines to write down your weaknesses and pray for forgiveness.

_____

_____

_____

_____

In case you do not know **how to pray**, Jesus gave us a model prayer in Matthew 6:9-13 and again in Luke 11:2-4. God knew our need of how to pray. I would dare say that most of us that have grown up in the church know the Lord's Prayer by memory. Do you use this prayer as a guide when you pray? In Matthew 6:6, we are told to get into our prayer room and shut the door. I'm reminded of a recent movie, "War Room," and according to news media, the internet, and other sources, many individuals went home to develop their own prayer room. God knew we needed to be removed from all interaction with the world so that we could speak to God and he could speak to us. We do not need our cell phones, TV, or any other device or person that might hinder our worship, praise, or petitions. I'm guilty of neglecting this one at times as I tend to pray on the run.

When I was teaching, I would pray almost all the way to work for the twenty-six miles it took to get there. There were days I would marvel that I got to work as I didn't remember a single red light on the way. There are fifteen red lights between my house and the school in which I taught. Subsequently, there would definitely be distractions. I could not give God my total attention! Now that I am retired, it is easier to get on my knees or find the time to enter into God's presence without worldly distractions. Hold it! I just took a selfie! I could have gotten up fifteen minutes earlier to have that quiet time if I had only planned to do so. I have no excuse! I was selfish. I wanted fifteen more minutes of sleep. Wow, not exactly what I wanted to share. But, I'm sure you may find conviction as well. We all need to make time for praying to Jesus! It could be that your schedule is such that you need to get up fifteen minutes earlier. You may also need to take at least five minutes of your lunch time in prayer. When you teach middle school, you need to pray without ceasing! And all teachers, said, "AMEN!" The Psalmist knew we needed to pray at noon and gave us the example to challenge us to get our hearts right with the Lord. Hence, we need to pray before we go to bed. Many nights I go to sleep saying my prayers. It is then that I pray the Holy Spirit is interceding on my behalf! I have given up watching the nightly news because so much of it is negative and depressing. Instead, my husband and I will discuss the day and the things we are thankful for and make plans for a more productive tomorrow.

Again let me assure you that God knows our needs. He knows that our sinful nature leads us into situations that take us away from Him. He knows we need to pray about this thought continually. "When He came to the place, He said to them, "Pray that you may not enter into temptation." (Luke 22:40 NKJV) God placed it in our model prayer and again throughout scriptures to remind us how important it is. We must not cease to pray for our deliverance from temptation.

In order to do this, we need to put on the whole armor of God. Ephesians 6:10-18 gives us the picture of cladding a soldier prepared for combat. Please get a Bible and read it. I will paraphrase it by relating we are to first be strong in the Lord by calling upon His power and might. In order to stand against the devil, we must put on the breastplate of righteousness. We must gird our waist with the truth. We must shod our feet with the gospel of peace. It tells us that above all, we need to take the shield of faith with us to quench all the fiery darts of the wicked one (the devil.) Accordingly, we are to take the helmet of salvation and the sword of the Spirit (the Word of God.) Paul finishes in verse eighteen by saying, "praying always with all prayer and supplication in the Spirit, being watchful to this end with all perseverance and supplication for all the saints—"(NKJV) The **Truth** is stated again. We are to pray always! We are to pray in the Spirit for ourselves and for other Christians. Holding to these truths, there is the word—watchful. We must watch over our weaknesses with the help of Jesus. I mentioned before that in Luke 22:44 we are to pray in earnest. It is that intense sincere prayer that Jesus loves. Those are the ones that allow Jesus to heal our infirmities. He told us so in scripture. Will you claim His healing? You can if you believe and call on the name of Jesus.

[20]"So Jesus said to them, "Because of your unbelief; for assuredly, I say to you, if you have faith as a mustard seed, you will say to this mountain, 'Move from here to there,' and it will move; and nothing will be impossible for you." [21]However, this kind does not go out except by prayer and fasting." (Matthew 17:20-21 NKJV) We are disciples of Jesus. He was saying this truth to all His disciples then and now. If we really want the power of the Lord, then we must be willing to pray earnestly and fast. Jesus gave us this example. I have not fasted as often as I should in my Christian walk. I have participated in fasting and prayer. If you recall the story I told earlier, when our Bible

study ladies went to the lady of our church who had cancer, we all committed to fasting before we went. We went expecting a miracle of healing for our friend. We prayed in the name of Jesus for healing and anointed her with oil. Our friend received that miracle of healing. God blessed a whole community and many others were saved as a result of that miracle. The joy that comes from participating in God's work is indescribable! It is my prayer that you learn to fast and pray so you will experience the power that only God can give. I would love for you to e-mail me your stories of the miracles you experience as a result. Your joy will be overflowing and you will want to share that joy! I would love to include these in my next book. Please send me your stories.

Another truth is that we are to ask others to pray for us. "Brethren, pray for us." (1 Thessalonians 4:14 NKJV) We are to pray for others and we are to ask others to pray for us. It is essential we understand we cannot go it alone. That is why Jesus said to not forsake the assembling of the saints. God knew we needed each other. He created us as social beings as well as spiritual beings. It is important we solicit prayer warriors who will in turn lift us up. I have several Godly women who lift me up in prayer daily. Lord knows, I need it! You may chuckle here, but it is the truth. "Beloved, I pray that you may prosper in all things and be in health, just as your soul prospers." (3 John 1:2 NKJV) John knew that he needed to pray for his friends to not only do well, but to prosper in all things. That is better than to just do well. It is to flourish and thrive. It is to succeed. And yes, it is to show a profit. Not just in finances, but more importantly, in health. Our health is the most important physical asset we possess. Without good health, there is little we can do. Once again, we can see the importance of having others pray for us. Don't allow another day to go by without you finding someone that will commit to pray for you and your health.

We do have several needs that we must pray for daily so our lives will be complete. We first need to pray for our relatives and close friends. We have a need to pray for them to prosper in all things. Second, we need to pray about how to discipline our children. There are many scriptures to help you as you learn to discipline those you love. Third, you need to pray about something that may seem taboo to you. You and your husband need to pray and discuss your sexual needs. This is one area where couples can literally cause a breakdown in the marriage if not addressed. There are plenty of Christian authors out there that address this issue. Stormie Omartian addresses this issue in Chapter four of her book, "The Power of a Praying Wife."[3] I encourage you to read it. If this is an area of concern in your life, please seek out Christian authors who give wonderful insight on how to improve this area of your life. Fourth, you also need to pray about your finances. Too many of us purchase things because we "want" them and not because we need them. We feel the need to have what our neighbor may have. Consequently, we wonder why we can't pay the bills. I'm reminded of a couple my husband was counseling many years ago. They were not making ends meet. My husband asked them how many cigarettes they smoke collectively daily. She smoked one and a half packs a day. He smoked two packs a day. You may not know it, but the average pack of cigarettes cost $5.40 in Kentucky according to 2014 statistics.[4] Multiplied out—it is $6,898.50 a year! You do the math on this couple. No wonder they couldn't make ends meet. You may be spending money on cigarettes or other drugs without realizing how much you are wasting on a worldly pleasure that will only hurt your health. The first step is to realize you need prayer to beat this selfish habit. The next step is rather simple. Pray without ceasing. You must find something better to replace your habit. You will need to pray over what to replace that habit. My own father was addicted to a pipe. He was diagnosed with throat cancer in his sixties and was told to stop smoking. He immediately gave up the pipe and started chewing gum. Contrary to what his dentist claimed, the gum never caused one cavity and when he died at age ninety-two, he had all his teeth! The gum was a good replacement for his pipe smoking. Again, you will have to pray and seek with what you should replace your habit.

The fifth need you should pray about is your employment or need for employment. You need to be on your knees praying for the Lord's guidance in this area of your life. In the Bible, Paul gave us a Biblical Truth when he wrote in 2 Thessalonians 3: 10b ": If anyone will not work, neither shall he eat." (NKJV) There are too many people in this world who can work that want to selfishly take advantage of social programs. On the other hand, there are those who desperately need those programs to survive as they cannot work. However, there is work to be found not far from your fingertips in today's world. Computers and cell phones have made this possible. I'm sure you have heard statistics given by our government. They claim that for the first time in history we have only 49% of the people paying one-hundred per cent of the taxes in America. There is no clear answer to the problem. One way to alleviate this would be to teach our children a work ethic and then, model a prayer life dedicated to the Lord. Ask God to bless your work. He will direct and crown your efforts with success as promised in Proverbs.

I am choosing to close this chapter with a warning. "But the end of all things is at hand; therefore be serious and watchful in your prayers." (1 Peter 4: 7 NKJV) Our world is in serious chaos. At every turn, we can become discouraged by the events we hear and see on television, on Facebook, and the many other media outlets. There are videos on U-tube that espouse hatred and bigotry toward humankind of every nation. If beheading was not bad enough, we watched in horror as humans were burned alive! Yes, I earlier alluded to the fact that Jesus will come again and that no one knows the hour or the day. In 1 Peter, he compels us to be watchful in our prayers, and in verse eight, he commands us to have a fervent love for one another above all else. He denotes that love will cover a multitude of sins. We must learn to love our neighbor unconditionally. It does not mean we must accept their lifestyle or sins. It does mean we are to love them in spite of their sins and pray for them to realize their sin. We are to serve for God's glory—not ours. We are to become unselfish. We are to be hospitable to one another without grumbling. I remember a time at a church social when we were bringing in food for a potluck. One of the men was complimenting the ladies about their service. One lady spoke up rather harshly that it ought to be enough food because she slaved over six dishes that she brought! Finally, the man spoke up and said he was so thankful that she went above and beyond what she had to do. Another lady assured her that she would receive a blessing from all her efforts. The lady just turned and walked away without a word. It is easy for the devil to get into your mind and let you think you are more important than you are. There are some people who need to have their egos filled so they get their reward here on earth. We are to minister our gifts to one another without grumblings! We are to minister to others so that God may be glorified through Jesus Christ living in us. That is selflessness. It is nice to get earthly recognition. However, the REAL recognition we should seek is not here on earth but in heaven. To attain such a lofty goal, we must pray without ceasing. Be watchful of our attitudes. Our selfish nature can creep up on us so quickly!

One of my students had a whole bag of jolly ranchers he had brought to school one day. I overheard him telling his friends, "No, you can't have any of my candy." I walked over to him and asked him if he wasn't being a little selfish? He replied to me, "No ma'am, I'm just practical. If I give them my candy, then I don't have any for myself!" Exactly! Our attitudes are wrapped up in ourselves. Selfishness reigns. How do we overcome selfishness? We pray that Jesus would show us our selfish ways without ceasing. Remember, the Holy Spirit will intercede for you even when your flesh is weak. Use the model prayer Jesus gave us. Pray away all temptation. Remember to put on the whole armor of God and pray earnestly in God's will. We may be led to pray while fasting. When we fast, God will help us to "move mountains." Next, we are to pray for others to prosper and ask others to pray for us as well. Lastly, we are to serve for God's glory all the time being watchful that we do so in unconditional love for others. What is God asking you to do? Write down what you think God is calling you to do. What confessions do you need to make? Make a plan of action to get rid of selfishness in your life.

_____

_____

_____

_____

_____

_____

# Chapter Twelve

# Rejoice In The Lord, Always!

"Rejoice in the Lord always. Again I will say, rejoice!" (Philippians 4: 4 NKJV)

This is for you. Yes, rejoice! Why? Because when you rejoice, you cannot be sad or depressed. You must have a happy frame of mind to rejoice. Are you beginning to be happy? Again, I say—rejoice! What for? Because you have a God who loves you so much that He gave His one and only Son that you might be saved to rejoice! Are you rejoicing yet? You may feel downtrodden and discouraged. Don't give up! Instead, rejoice! Because Jesus has promised to feed you and clothe you and shelter you, **YOU** can rejoice. (Matthew 6:25-34 paraphrased.) If you are in a situation where you are reading this and you may be thinking, "That is a bunch of bull," then, you need to pick yourself up and seek out a Christian brother or sister to help you. There are many out here willing to help and rejoice with you. Those of you who are reading this and are Christians—be perceptive of those who need your help and rejoice when they are found!

In the Bible, Luke gives us a beautiful picture of a man who had a hundred sheep and one went astray. The man went out to find it and upon finding the sheep, he placed it upon his shoulders and rejoiced. Luke 15:6 exclaims, "And when he comes home, he calls together his friends and neighbors, saying to them, 'Rejoice with me, for I have found my sheep which is lost!'." Please read this story again. Notice that the man placed his lost sheep on his shoulders. You and I are called to carry the burden of someone who is lost. We must seek them out. We must engage our lives with their lives. Is it easy? No, but it is so rewarding! You will rejoice! There are enemies along the way to keep you from finding lost souls. Back then, wolves and other vermin caused concern for the shepherd. Today, it is often social media and all the worldly pleasures in which we can become involved.

Do you know your neighbors so well that you invite them to your church? What keeps you from coming to Jesus and going and telling His story? What keeps you from witnessing to the lost? I believe it boils down to being afraid to step out on faith. I believe it is a lack of growth to get to the commitment you need to serve. However, you and I can rejoice. 1 Thessalonians 5:16 simply states, "Rejoice always," (NKJV) Paul knew that even in prison, he could rejoice in the Lord. Can you rejoice, yet? Are you in prison to things of this world? Don't delay. Involve someone in praying for you to escape the prison you have set for yourself and then, rejoice! Here are a few lines for you to write down what keeps you from rejoicing. Write down the things that lock you away from rejoicing. Give them to Jesus and He will free you to rejoice!

---

The Psalmist penned it beautifully in Psalms 33:1, "Rejoice in the Lord, O you righteous! For praise from the upright is beautiful." Think about it. The heavens love to hear our rejoicing. You and I need to start each day with rejoicing. When we do this, we become thankful for the many blessings we experience. It takes away our selfish nature. Through rejoicing, you can overcome that selfish desire that prevents you from living a joy-filled life. In Romans 12:15a you are implored to, "Rejoice with those who rejoice. . ." When two or more are rejoicing over their blessings, how can there be any negative? How can there be any fear? You cannot be depressed! You can have success! Rejoice!!

While studying an on-line Bible study one day, I came across three qualities for joyful, effective ministry from Paul Tripp Ministries. In his study, he admonishes the church because it should be the most forgiving community on earth.[5] Yet, I'm sure you may have witnessed how unforgiving some church members can be. My husband and I personally witnessed unforgiving church members in almost every church we've ever worked. That is why in the scriptures that Paul reminded us that we have all sinned and come short of the glory of God. (Romans 3:23)

Please allow me to give an example where serving the Lord can cause persecution, yet you can rejoice. A few years ago, David was approached to preach at a church near our community. He preached a few times and was then asked to consider preaching on a more permanent basis. Much prayer was lifted up for several weeks as David and I considered many factors affecting ourselves, other churches and people we loved greatly. Just as we had decided to serve the Lord in this new church, we also discovered that two people within that church had taken great effort to squelch David's becoming the full-time minister. We were humbled to have been sought, and yet excited to serve the Lord in the new church, only to have been rejected quite cruelly. We learned that those two people had been responsible for calling in many members who no longer attended to vote against the call. Shocked, we prayed and sought God's guidance on what had just happened. We didn't know the intentions of those who hurt us and we didn't listen to gossip and hearsay. Instead, we rejoiced in the Lord! We knew God had a more perfect plan for our lives. We prayed for those who persecuted us and completely forgave them. We trusted Jesus to lead us. We rejoiced!

A year later, we were called to a small church that desperately needed us and our willingness for outreach. We are presently serving in the young church with the sweetest congregation. God is expanding His kingdom in our church. This does not mean it is without growth pains and difficulties. As we trust in the Lord and lean not on our own understanding, this too will pass. They are willing to grow and go for Jesus. We have seen the congregation triple in size and everyone is rejoicing! They have a forgiving and a loving spirit! Everyone who comes into our church is amazed at how we welcome them into our fellowship. We rejoice! God is so good!

Paul Tripp discussed in his Bible study about three areas of strife that occurs between our heart and God's heart—"grief, zeal, and grace."[6] He explains how the church should be the saddest community because we should be grieving over the lost. Do you grieve and pray over someone you know is lost? God gave us the power of free choice but sin robbed us of what was meant to be beautiful. From the beginning, we were to be constant companions with God in the Garden of Eden. When we chose the tree of knowledge, we became selfish individuals that cast blame on each other. As we look at Adam and Eve, we too, come up with all kinds of stories to justify our actions. Our **selfish** ways prevail. Each of us should be grieving over all the lost souls with whom we come in contact daily. Some of them are family members and some are counted as good friends. There are others who we work with or are acquaintances. Yet, we can lift up our hearts and rejoice. How? We can put words into action for Jesus. We can show a positive influence on our children and grandchildren by reading them the Word of God and praying with them. Let them see us rejoice in the Lord. This is the zeal that Tripp spoke of.[7] Zeal is God's plan that through our daily living others can hear and see the Gospel of salvation through us. Can others see Jesus in how you live your life daily? We must live our life rejoicing! Again, we must guard our hearts from the selfishness that would rob us of this influence on others. However, if we are zealous to love our neighbors as ourselves and reach the lost, we can rejoice in the joy we receive. My husband ends his sermons almost every Sunday with this quote, "You may be the only Jesus, Jesus living in you. . .that somebody sees this week." That is another reason we should go through our lives rejoicing.

The third area mentioned in Tripp's Bible study is grace.[8] In 2 Peter 3: 9 we see the grace of God is that God is not willing that any should perish. God wants all of us to come to repentance. What marvelous grace! Jesus was sent to wash away our sins—to be the blood sacrifice so that we would be covered from our filthiness. We can truly rejoice that God made a way for the "worse" sinner to come into His kingdom. That is something to rejoice about! No matter what you have done in the past or what you are presently doing that you know is wrong, you can rejoice that God will forgive you when you ask. Through Jesus, we can live peacefully with everyone. We are to pray for those who spitefully use us. We are to overcome evil with good. That type of living is a cause to rejoice. No matter what this world can do to us, we can rejoice! Our reward is not on this earth—it is in heaven. The verse from John 16:22 points to our ultimate joy, "Therefore you now have sorrow; but I will see you again and your heart will rejoice, and your joy no one will take from you." (NKJV) Wow! Jesus will return and our hearts will rejoice. No one can take that joy from you. No one can take that joy from me. We can rejoice!

Rejoice, in the Lord always! Again, I say rejoice. We are called to tell others about the love of Jesus. It is my prayer that you will not run away from God's calling. It is your choice. There is so much joy that you will experience when you answer God's call. God is there to give each of us hope. Yes, God gives hope to selfish, lazy, hypocritical humans like me and you! Rejoice in that hope and claim it! You can overcome selfishness with God's help. To do this, you must renew your mind daily in God's Word and then share His love with others. I am still struggling on a daily basis to overcome selfishness. I must pray without ceasing to overcome my thoughtless choice of words when in conversation with my husband or others. I will rejoice when I can remember events or wisely choose my words. That is the way it should be. Remember, we must ask others to pray with us to succeed over our selfish ways and the world. It is my prayer you succeed! Our world depends on your success. "Rejoice in the Lord, Always! Again, I say rejoice!"

There are many of you who are living in pain without complaining and instead, with joy in your hearts. My sister's husband, Al, was one such person. My brother-in-law was stricken with polio during his service in the Air Force. He was one of the lucky ones that walked again, as a few of his fellow servicemen had their lives cut short due to a bad batch of live polio virus. Did you know that thirty years from the time someone gets polio; it frequently strikes the body again? This time, polio put Al into a motorized wheelchair and eventually he was bed ridden. Tragically, in the last years of his life, the only time Al was out of bed was if a caretaker helped him into a wheelchair. Toward the end, only a lift could get him out of bed. All the times we visited him, I never heard him complain. He could not get up and come into the dining room to eat with his family or friends for the last years of his life. In those years, Al could have been bitter and yelled and screamed at the people who were caregivers. He was in extreme amounts of pain. His caregivers said that he never complained. It seemed he had a peace about his circumstances in life. I'm sure there are those reading this book that can identify. You can have that peace that passes all understanding too. (Philippians 4:7 paraphrased) There are so many service men and women who exemplify their faith. Here are a few lines for you to write about your fears and ask God to give you the peace that only He can give. Also, for those of you that need to ask Jesus into your heart, write a few lines to express your gratitude for what Jesus did for you on Calvary's cross. Write down your greatest shortcomings and ask God to show you a way to leave them behind. Then, be silent and listen. Be ready to write down what God has placed on your heart.

_____

_____

_____

_____

_____

_____

Are you praising the Lord yet? In Psalm 106:1 the Psalmist exclaimed, "Praise the Lord! Oh, give thanks to the Lord, for He is good! His mercy endures forever." (NKJV) Make a list of at least five things that you can Praise the Lord for:

_____

_____

_____

_____

_____

_____

Well. . .this is my last chapter. However, I am leaving you with many scriptures that follow for you to study and hide in your heart. I have shared with you my Christian "selfie!" As you can see, I have had many mountaintop experiences with Jesus and I have been in the valleys with Jesus as well. Like I stated before, I am no different than most of you. I still catch myself being selfish! That fact is why I wrote a self-help book. I can daily read and reread what I need to work through to avoid selfishness. Now it is time for you to write your journey with the Lord. The scriptures that follow will help you to walk with Jesus if you just memorize and carry them in your heart. Again, I challenge you to do this in the name of Jesus! May God bless you as you write and live your Christian "Selfie!"

# Scriptures To Study and "Hide In Your Heart"

O ver the years, while searching scriptures to lead Bible studies and my own personal studies, I have come to depend on several scriptures that I pray will become a blessing to you. There are too many to make a list of them all. However, I have already used many of them in this book. Here are a few more that you can use as a Bible study. I have used them to guide me in overcoming my selfish nature. They also give me great comfort and joy to know I am not alone in the pursuit of God's heart. All of these scriptures come from the New King James Version and I have again included a few lines to give you a chance to use them as a Bible study. God has given us such a great gift—the gift of salvation. While some people think that their "good works" will amount for something and others think "I am a good person," none of these will gain an entrance into heaven. That is why the first verse you should study deals with the grace God has given us as sinners.

"[8] For by grace you have been saved through faith, and that not of yourselves; it is the gift of God, [9]not of works, lest anyone should boast."(Ephesians 2: 8-9 NKJV) Write a definition of grace. What makes this a gift? What does it mean, ". . .not of works?"

_____

_____

_____

"Nor is there salvation in any other, for there is no other name under heaven given among men by which we must be saved." (Acts 4: 12 NKJV) What is the name by which we are saved? Write here a statement of rejoicing if you are saved. If not, ask for Jesus to forgive you?

_____

_____

_____

"Do you not know that you are the temple of God and that the Spirit of God dwells in you?" (1 Corinthians 3: 16 NKJV) What do you know about the Holy Spirit? Find more scriptures that support you having the Holy Spirit within you. Can you be selfish if the Holy Spirit is in you?

_____

_____

_____

"Be diligent to present yourself approved to God, a worker who does not need to be ashamed, rightly dividing the word of truth." (2 Timothy 2: 15 NKJV) Why should you read God's Word daily? How can memorizing scripture give you confidence? Why is this important?

_____

_____

_____

"16All Scripture is given by inspiration of God, and is profitable for doctrine, for reproof, for correction, for instruction in righteousness, 17that the man of God may be complete, thoroughly equipped for every good work." (2 Timothy 3: 16-17 NKJV) What does this verse say to you? Are you reading and memorizing God's Word? Write down a time you will study God's Word.

_____

_____

_____

"My little children, let us not love in word or in tongue, but in deed and in truth." (1 John 3: 18 NKJV) Make a list of how you can show love to others.

_____

_____

_____

"I have shown you in every way, by laboring like this, that you must support the weak. And remember the words of the Lord Jesus, that He said, It is more blessed to give than to receive." (Acts 20: 35 NKJV) Why do we work? Are you supporting anyone? Why are government programs harmful to society? What do you tithe? Pray about it.

_____

_____

_____

"No one, when he has lit a lamp, puts it in a secret place or under a basket, but on a lampstand, that those who come in may see the light." (Luke 11: 33 NKJV) What does this verse mean to you? Are you letting others see the light of Jesus in you? Write down how.

_____

_____

_____

"⁴Abide in Me and I in you. As the branch cannot bear fruit of itself, unless it abides in the vine, neither can you, unless you abide in Me. ⁵I am the vine, you are the branches. He who abides in Me, and I in Him, bears much fruit; for without Me you can do nothing." Dwell on this truth and write what it can mean for your life. Are you bearing fruit? Write what you can do:

_____

_____

_____

"Therefore, whatever you want me to do to you, do also to them, for this is the Law and the Prophets." (Matthew 7: 12 NKJV) Make a list of how you want to be treated. Is this an area where you have been selfish? If so, ask God to reveal this to you and ask for forgiveness.

_____

_____

_____

"But those that wait on the Lord Shall renew their strength; They shall mount up with wings like eagles, They shall run and not be weary, They shall walk and not faint." (Isaiah 40: 31 NKJV) What are ways in which you can wait on God? Are you anxious? How can you claim this verse?

_____

_____

_____

One of my very favorite Psalms is Psalms 95: 1 because I love to sing praises to the Lord. It says, "Oh come, let us sing to the Lord! Let us shout joyfully to the Rock of our salvation." We will be singing and praising God for all eternity. You may not be able to carry a tune here on earth, but in heaven you will sing beautifully! Rejoice!

I would love to share with you all my favorite Proverbs, but there are just too many. Please take the challenge to read at least one or two daily. Then, try to recall the verses the next day. If you cannot, go back and reread them. It is a great way to change your attitudes and life. It will also help you fight against selfish desires.

I lift up my final favorite verse from the Old Testament as a challenge as well. Commit this verse to memory as the last days seem to be even closer than I could ever imagine. I believe this promise and that is why I am sharing it again. God will heal our land! We must pray it collectively. It is plural and not singular. All Christians must pray this daily and believe God will hear. It is His will. This is prayer that God will answer if we just give it to Him and believe. Rejoice!

"If my people who are called by My name will humble themselves, and pray and seek My face, and turn from their wicked ways, then I will hear from heaven, and will forgive their sin and heal their land." (1 Chronicles 7: 14 NKJV)

What a promise! Then, why are we not humbling ourselves and claiming God's victory? It is called selfishness. We have become a nation of political correctness. There is a selfish attitude that pervades the nation more than any other time since its beginning. It seems that we are becoming a nation of entitlement, whether it is through government programs or the workplace where it appears the attitude has become, "We deserve more." Unfortunately, I have heard of teachers who took laptop computers home to use and never returned them to the school. They felt "entitled" to the perks of a trade. The behavior of entitlement has become evident in every walk of life. This behavior is wrong. It is called selfishness!

We can still rejoice and give God the glory. We need to lift up this verse every day. If enough of us earnestly pray, God has promised to answer and heal our land from our selfish ways. God can give us back the America where we had prayer in schools. God can heal our land. God will heal our selfish ways. Rejoice in the Lord! Again, I say rejoice! May God bless you and may God bless America!

P.S. Now that you have taken your selfie, what does Jesus see?

# Acknowledgements

For all my friends and family who gave me encouragement, I want to thank you. Most of you did not realize how I relied on a simple word of praise to lift my spirits.

Words cannot express how thankful I am for my daughters, Laura and Lisa, who helped me through a major identity crisis with the order of events in my writing this book. They have been my tireless "angels" working to bring creative ideas that help make my direction and purpose more clear. Thank you also to my daughter, Leslie for her support. May God bless all your efforts and families for staying up late helping me take that constant "selfie."

I am truly thankful to have my partner, my husband of forty-four years, encourage and become my inspiration to write once again. He became my constant cheerleader and fact finder. May God bless you! We grew stronger as you shared ways I could work on selfish habits. For your support and reassurance I rejoice!

Thank you, Bobbie Rodriguez, who believed in me and took an ugly duckling and gave me the wings of a swan. Jennifer Kasper, you are so kind to someone who never meets a deadline! You hung in there with me through all of my mistakes. Thank you to Xulon Press and the rest of the staff who edited, shaped and labored over the production of my book. All of you have been a true blessing.

Most of all, I want to Praise the Lord for His inspiring Words! Thank you, Jesus for allowing me to become your vessel to lift You up and Praise Your Holy Name! May Your Words in this book not return void! Amen!

# End Notes

Chapter 4

[1]Holley Gerth. *You're Going To Be Okay.* (Revell. A division of Baker Publishing Group. 2014), 121.

[2]Ibid. 121.

Chapter 11

[3]Stormie Omartian. *The Power of a Praying Wife.* (Harvest House Publishers, 1997), 61-67.

[4]"What a Pack of Cigarettes Costs, State By State." *The AWL.* August 1, 2014, http://www.theawl.com.

Chapter 12

[5]Paul Tripp Ministries,Inc. *"Three Areas of Strife Between Our Heart's and God's Heart."* (blog), February 25, 2015, http://www. info@paultripp.com.

[6]Ibid. (pages unnumbered on blog)

[7]Ibid. (pages unnumbered on blog)

[8]Ibid. (pages unnumbered on blog)

CPSIA information can be obtained
at www.ICGtesting.com
Printed in the USA
LVOW12s1357121216

516916LV00002B/66/P